THE KINGFISHER

EXTREME NATURE ENCYCLOPEDIA

KINGFISHER

First published in 2026 by Kingfisher
a division of Macmillan Children's Books
The Smithson, 6 Briset Street, London, EC1M 5NR
EU representative: Macmillan Publishers Ireland Ltd, 1st Floor,
The Liffey Trust Centre, 117–126 Sheriff Street Upper,
Dublin 1 D01 YC43
Associated companies throughout the world

ISBN 978-1-0350-8877-5

Authors: Anna Claybourne, Richard Mead, Will Potter, Cath Senker
Editor: Alicia Williamson
Project Manager: Claire Lister
Consultant: Tom Jackson
Design: Dynamo Limited
Packaged by Dynamo Limited

1 3 5 7 9 8 6 4 2
1TR/0426/WKT/RV/128MA

A CIP catalogue record for this book is available from the British Library.

Printed in China

NOTE TO READERS: The facts and statistics in this edition are accurate as of January 2026.

MIX
Paper | Supporting responsible forestry
FSC www.fsc.org
FSC® C116313

THE KINGFISHER

EXTREME NATURE ENCYCLOPEDIA

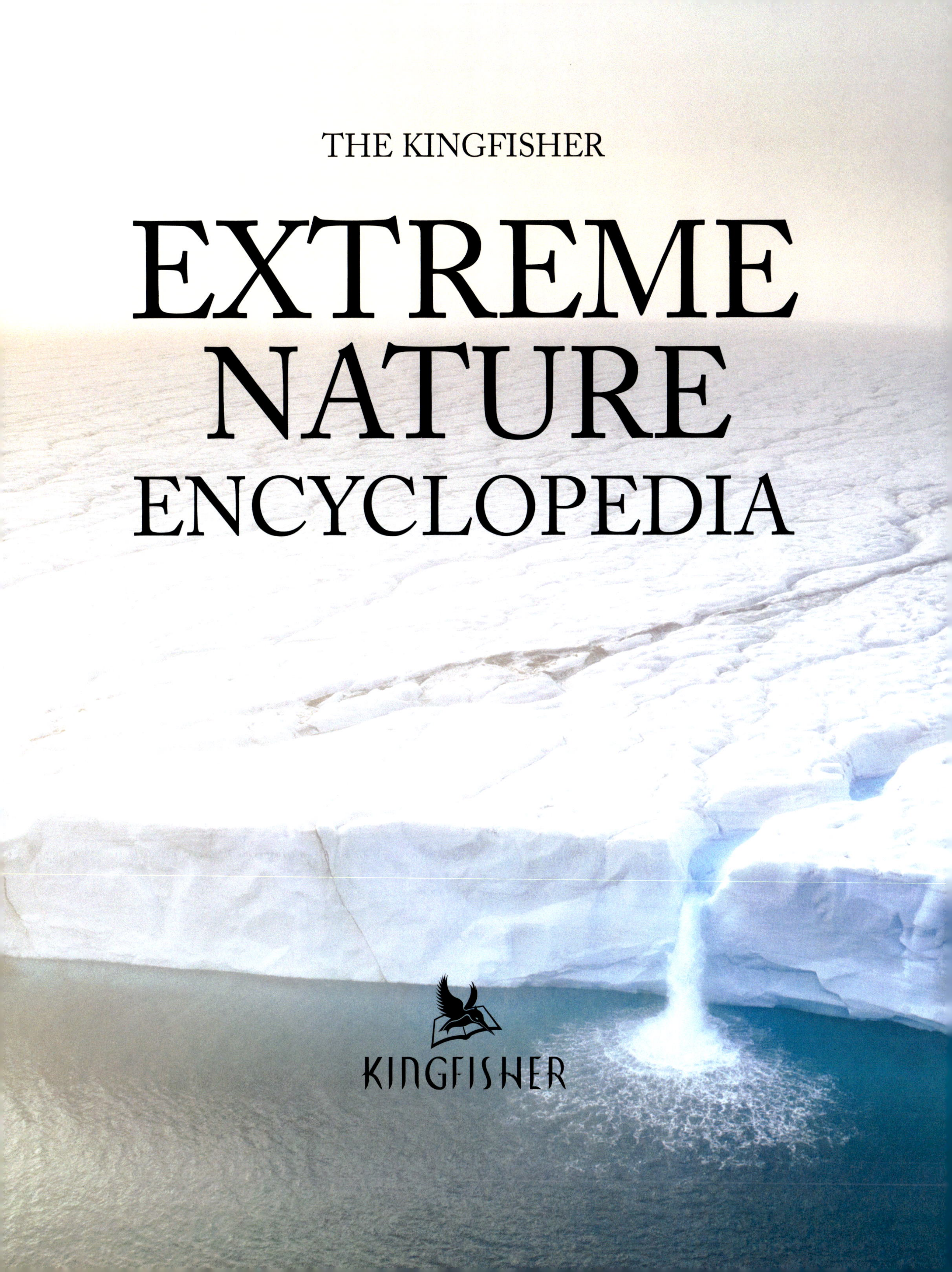

KINGFISHER

CONTENTS

CHAPTER FOUR: DANGEROUS WINDS

CHAPTER FIVE: EXTREME WATER

CHAPTER SIX: PREPARING FOR THE FUTURE

REFERENCES:

INTRODUCTION

Our planet is the only one we know of that has exactly the right conditions to support life, but Earth still presents some severe challenges to the plants and animals that call it home. Nature can be extreme, with phenomena that are thrilling and awe-inspiring on the one hand and terrifying and massively destructive on the other. The *Kingfisher Extreme Nature Encyclopedia* explores natural distasters and weather at their most intense to help you understand how and why these events occur.

The encyclopedia is divided into six parts. The first chapter, 'Geological Disasters', looks at natural disasters related to rocks and the shifting tectonic plates that make up Earth's outer layer. You'll find information about everything from earthquakes to space rocks in this section.

Chapters two and three deal with extreme heat and cold, examining how our atmosphere can create scorching and freezing conditions that can bring droughts and wildfires or ice storms and avalanches.

The fourth chapter, 'Extreme Winds', explains how winds work and spotlights the most powerful winds on Earth – found in spinning cyclones and tornadoes.

The fifth section explores intense water-related events, from monsoons to rogue waves. It even has information on the strangest rains on record, with bizarre objects mixed into the precipitation!

The last part turns to what people are doing today to address the challenges presented by Earth's extremes. Human activities are making the extremes more frequent and severe, but new technologies and programmes are seeking to lessen the damage.

The *Kingfisher Extreme Nature Encyclopedia* is filled with fascinating phenomena and insights into Earth at its wildest, giving readers the chance to appreciate and prepare for the extremes.

◀ *Tropical Cyclone Batsirai approaches the coast of Madagascar with winds blowing at speeds of 235 km/h (145 mph). Taken in February 2022, this image showing the structure of the powerful storm was captured by a NASA-NOAA satellite.*

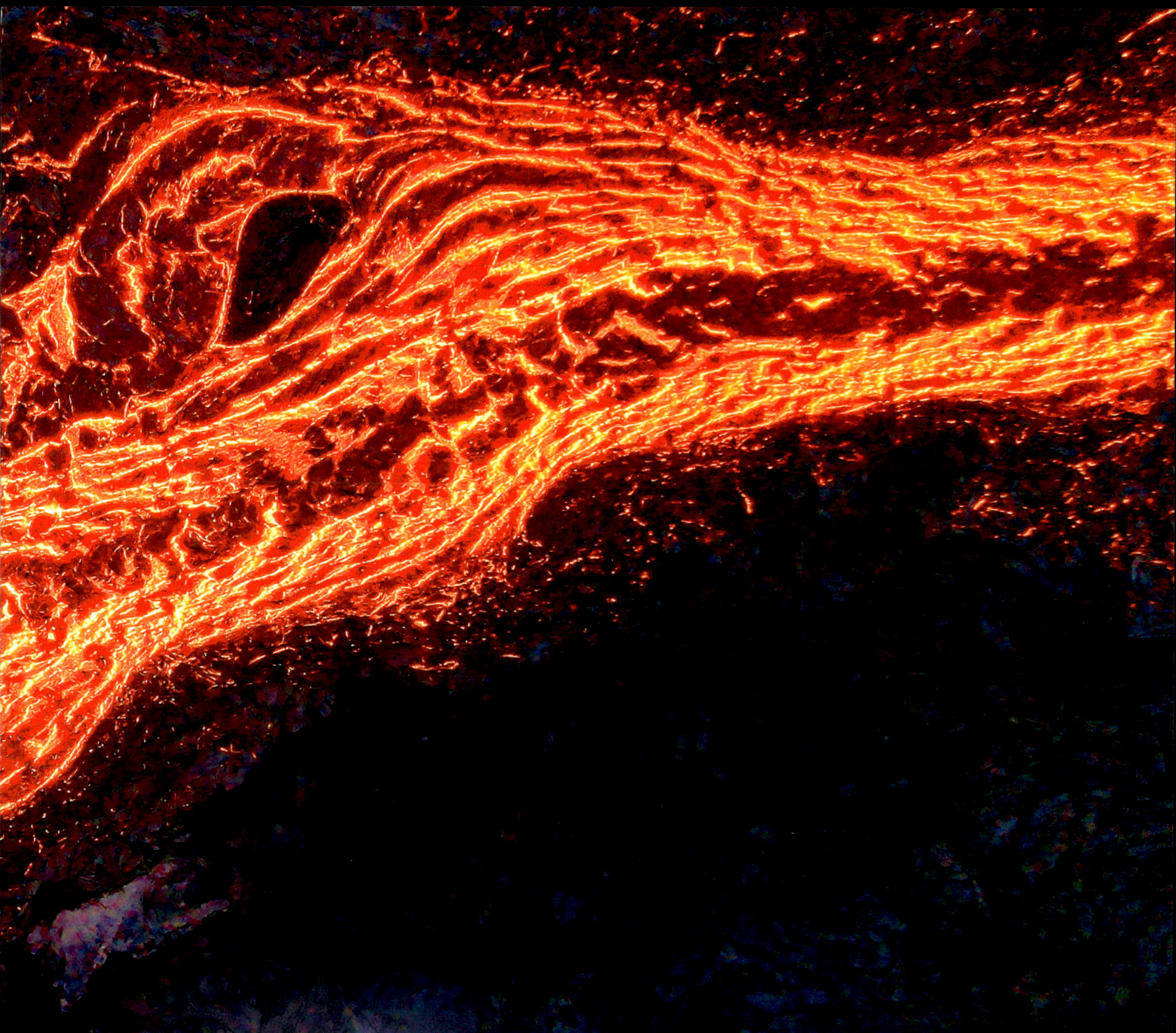

1 GEOLOGICAL DISASTERS

PLATE TECTONICS

The planet usually feels solid and fixed under our feet. However, it's actually made up of huge, moving sections, called tectonic plates.

These plates make up the hard, outer part of Earth known as the lithosphere. It is comprised of the crust, or outer layer of solid rock, and the uppermost part of the mantle, a thick layer of hot, partly melted rock. The mantle swirls around very slowly, and this makes the plates move too. Normally, this movement is so slow, we don't notice it at all. The plates move only about as fast as our fingernails grow!

PLATE BOUNDARIES

Plate boundaries are the places where the world's tectonic plates meet and touch each other. As you can see on the map, there are plate boundaries all over the world. They form long, jagged lines where the plates fit together like jigsaw pieces. Most plate boundaries are under the sea, but there are some on land as well.

At plate boundaries, the plates can scrape and push against each other, which can sometimes cause earthquakes. Volcanoes are more common at plate boundaries too. The movement of plates creates gaps and weaknesses in the crust at boundaries that allows magma (melted rock) from inside Earth to come closer to the surface. Scientists study the boundaries carefully to help understand what is happening deep inside Earth and how it affects the surface.

BOUNDARY TYPES

Scientists divide plate boundaries into several types, depending on the way the plates move. Around the world, different plates are moving in different directions. That means that in some places they push into each other while in others, they pull apart or slide sideways.

DIVERGENT PLATE BOUNDARY

CONVERGENT PLATE BOUNDARY

TRANSFORM PLATE BOUNDARY

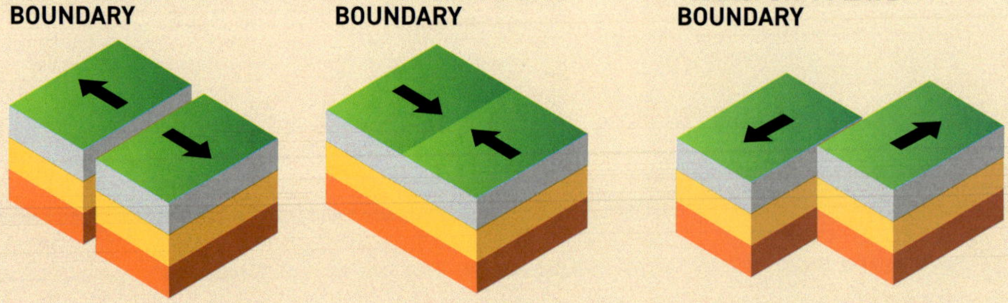

▲ *The plates move apart, and new crust forms between them.*

▲ *The plates push together. Usually, one slides underneath the other.*

▲ *The plates move in opposite directions and slide past each other.*

▼ *This world map shows the plates and the plate boundaries, with arrows showing which way each plate is moving.*

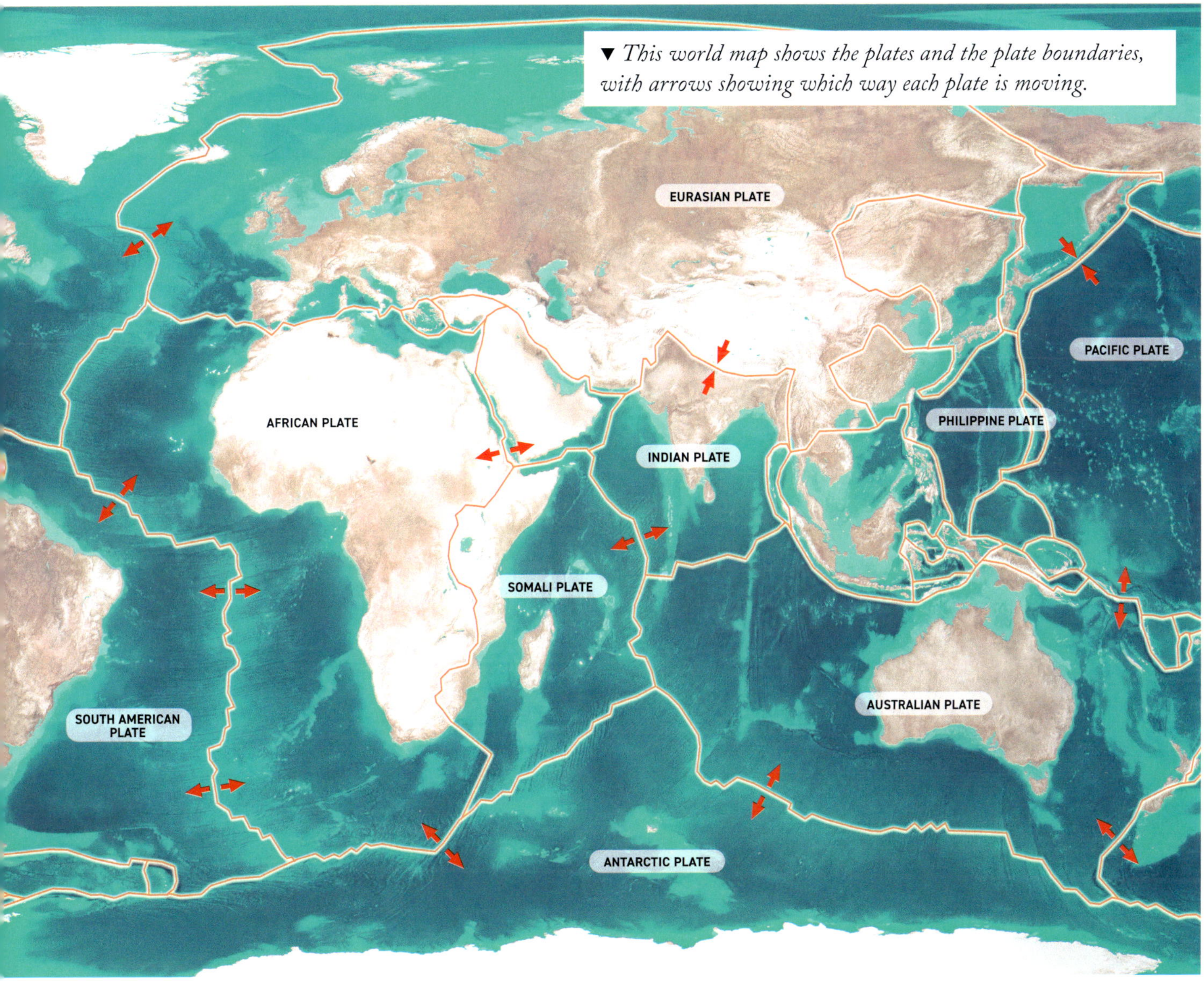

WHERE THREE PLATES MEET

In eastern Africa, there's a junction between three plates, the Nubian Plate, Somali Plate and Arabian Plate. They are all moving away from each other, and in the middle, a very small plate has formed, the Danakil Microplate. It rotates on its own, separately from the three main plates around it. This is making Earth's crust stretch out and get thinner, meaning the hot magma underground is very close to the surface. As a result, this area has a lot of volcanic eruptions and natural hot springs.

▲ *The Danakil Depression, part of the Danakil Microplate, is one of the lowest, hottest places on land.*

MID-ATLANTIC RIDGE

This very long, divergent plate boundary lies between the North and South American Plates to the west, and the African and Eurasian Plates to the east. It runs right through the island of Iceland, where it causes volcanic eruptions and geysers – fountains of boiling water heated by underground magma. Iceland uses the hot underground rock as a source of energy for geothermal (meaning 'Earth heat') power stations that turn heat into electricity.

However, most of the Mid-Atlantic Ridge is underwater, running down the middle of the Atlantic Ocean. As the plates pull apart, volcanic eruptions pour lava (erupted magma) out, which forms new seabed, making the Atlantic slightly wider each year.

▶ *A volcanic eruption at Geldingadalir in Iceland, with hot, molten lava bursting out from underground.*

HIMALAYAS

The Himalayas, in south Asia, are the world's biggest and highest mountain range. They formed about 50 million years ago, thanks to the movement of tectonic plates. Before this, India was an island, separate from the rest of Asia. But as the Indian Plate moved northwards, it slowly made India crash into Asia. At this convergent boundary, the Indian Plate pushed underneath the Eurasian Plate, making the land fold, crumple and rise up into giant mountains. These two plates are still pushing together today, and the Himalayas are growing higher, by about 5–10 mm every year.

▼ *A view of part of the Himalayas showing its permanently snow-capped peaks. The Himalayan mountain range includes Mount Everest, the world's highest mountain.*

SAN ANDREAS FAULT

This faultline is a famous transform plate boundary, where two plates slide against each other in opposite directions. It runs along the edge of North America, between the Pacific Plate (moving north) and the North American Plate (moving south). As the plates move, they sometimes get stuck and locked together. This makes tension build up until the plates suddenly slip, causing an earthquake. There have been several powerful earthquakes in this area, which have sometimes affected big cities like San Francisco, San Jose and Los Angeles.

▶ *A big crack in a road in Santa Cruz, California, caused by the Loma Prieta earthquake in 1989.*

▲ *At the Carrizo Plain, north of Los Angeles, you can see the San Andreas Fault as a scar or rift in the ground.*

EARTHQUAKES

Every day, there are more than 50 earthquakes around the world. But most of them are very weak, so we don't notice them.

Usually, it's only big, powerful earthquakes that cause disasters. These dangerous quakes mainly happen along the boundaries between the world's tectonic plates (see page 10). Earthquakes are especially common around the coast of the Pacific Ocean, in places like Chile, California, Japan, China and Indonesia, as well as in parts of western and central Asia, such as Turkey and Iran.

HOW EARTHQUAKES HAPPEN

Most earthquakes happen when two plates suddenly slip or judder as they scrape and slide past each other, making the ground jolt and shake. The starting point of an earthquake is called the focus. It can be deep underground or near the surface. The energy released by the quake spreads out from here in waves. The epicentre is the point on the surface that is immediately above the focus.

A powerful earthquake can cause a range of problems. Buildings may crack, tilt or even collapse. The shaking can make soft, sandy ground behave like quicksand, so cars or houses sink into it. Quakes can crack roads and bridges apart and make trees and power lines fall down. Sometimes, they also trigger landslides or tsunamis.

DETECTING TREMORS

It's impossible to say exactly when or where an earthquake will happen. But scientists use instruments called seismographs to record the motion of the ground when an earthquake occurs. These tools are so sensitive that they can even detect tremors that are too small for humans to feel. They show them as patterns of zigzag lines (above). The bigger the quake, the taller the peaks of the zigzag line will be.

▲ *This 2024 earthquake in Japan damaged roads and knocked over lamp posts in the city of Wajima.*

MEASURING EARTHQUAKES

Earthquakes are given a number that describes how powerful they are on a scale – usually from 1 to 10, with 10 being the most destructive. We once used the Richter scale to measure the power of quakes. Scientists have now switched to a similar (but more accurate) method called the moment magnitude scale, identified with the letter M. For example, the 2025 Myanmar earthquake in the photo below measured about M7.8. The biggest earthquake ever recorded, which took place in Chile in 1960, was around M9.5. Scientists use seismographs, information from satellites, and other technology to measure exactly how much an earthquake has moved the ground and how much energy it contained.

▼ *Collapsed buildings in the city of Mandalay, Myanmar, after a powerful earthquake in March 2025.*

THE MOMENT MAGNITUDE SCALE

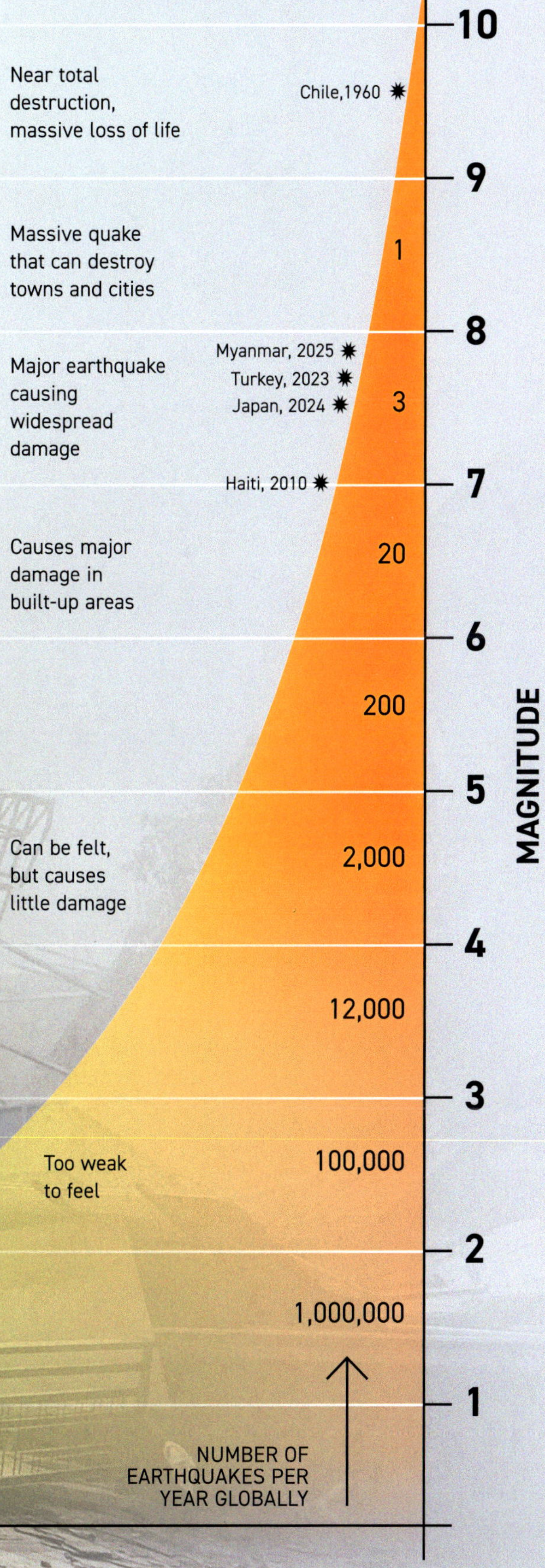

RESCUE AND RELIEF

When a big, dangerous earthquake strikes, rescuers rush to the area as fast as they can to help and rescue people. If roads are damaged or blocked by fallen trees or buildings, they may have to fly in by helicopter. They can also deliver emergency supplies of food, water and medicine by dropping parcels from planes. The most urgent job, however, is to find survivors who are trapped under collapsed buildings, often using machinery to free them.

▲ *Rescue dogs, such as this one that is being specially trained by Ukrainian emergency services in 2015, sniff out survivors and lead rescuers to where they are.*

▼ *A major earthquake in Turkey in 2023 caused widespread destruction, but lots of people were able to escape to safety from damaged buildings like these.*

VISUALISING QUAKES

When an earthquake happens, the ground shakes and moves for a few seconds or minutes, then stops. This makes it hard to show earthquakes and their effects on maps. Sometimes the epicentre of a quake is shown as a dot or star, with ripples or circles around it to show how far the shaking spreads out. Another way is to use colours. Red is usually used to show the most powerful shaking, close to the epicentre, fading to orange, yellow and green where the effects were weaker.

Some maps show locations of all the earthquakes that have happened in history, or over a particular time period. This type of map reveals which parts of the world are most prone to earthquake activity.

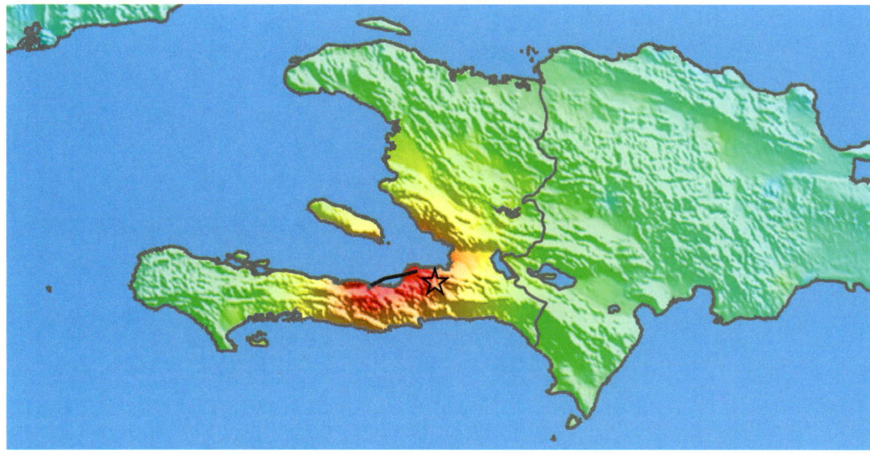

▲ *On this map of the 2010 Haiti earthquake, a star marks the epicentre, with the red area showing the most intense shaking.*

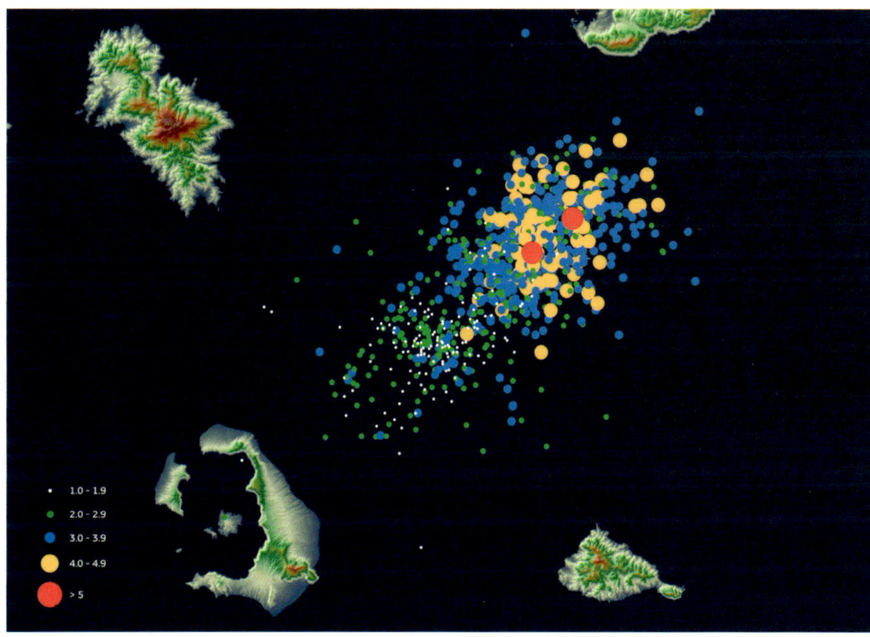

▶ *This map shows a 'seismic swarm', a series of seabed tremors that occurred over the course of ten days near the Greek island of Santorini in 2025. Bigger, brighter spots show the most powerful tremors.*

EARTHQUAKE-PROOF BUILDINGS

In earthquake-prone areas, modern buildings, especially tower blocks and skyscrapers, often have quake-resistant features to help them stay upright. Lightweight frameworks made of steel allow buildings to sway and flex instead of cracking (left). Some buildings are also built on base isolators (right), flexible foundations that absorb the movement, so that the building itself shakes less.

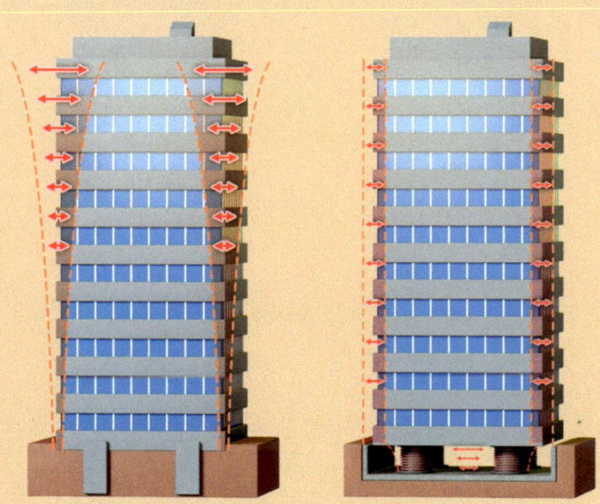

A CITY LEFT SHAKEN

On 28 March 2025, an M7.7 earthquake hit Myanmar near Mandalay, caused by the sudden slipping northwards of the Indian Plate along a fault. The quake caused widespread destruction, including the flattening of this residential tower block. Thousands were injured or lost their lives, while international rescue teams raced to save people trapped in the rubble.

TSUNAMI

A tsunami is an unusual kind of ocean wave that can sometimes cause disastrous floods and other damage when it reaches the land.

Tsunami is a Japanese word, meaning 'harbour wave'. This name came about because tsunamis only become obvious and destructive when they are close to land or a harbour. However, that's not where they start. A tsunami is created when something makes a large amount of water move suddenly in the ocean or a big lake. That could be an earthquake on the seabed, or sometimes a volcanic eruption causing a landslide that plunges into the sea. Because they are linked to earthquakes and volcanoes, tsunamis are mainly a problem close to tectonic plate boundaries around coasts and islands.

TSUNAMI DISASTERS

Tsunamis aren't always big, and don't always cause problems. Some tsunami waves are no bigger than normal ocean waves, and might even go unnoticed. But a large, powerful tsunami can cause a major disaster when it washes ashore, especially if it hits a built-up town or city area with lots of boats, buildings and people.

In movie posters and cartoons, a tsunami often looks like a giant, curved, breaking wave, but it's actually more like a wall of water rushing in over the land, or the sea level suddenly rising and surging onto the

shore. The fast-moving water can sweep away buildings, bridges, vehicles, trees, people and animals. Objects and debris floating around in the flood make it extra dangerous for anyone caught up in it. Tsunamis sometimes carry boats that were on the sea far inland, flatten and swamp fields of crops, and destroy clean water supplies.

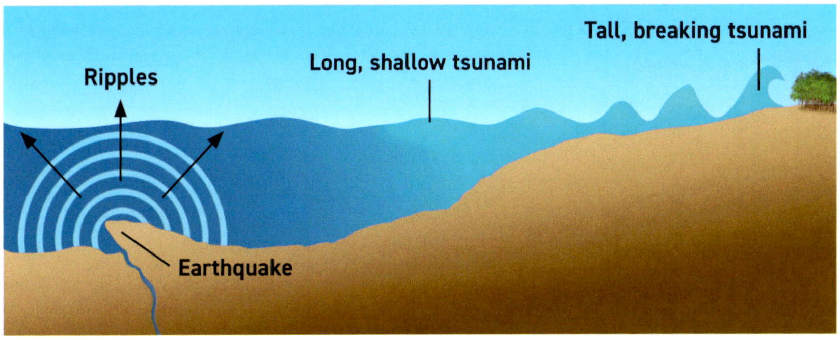

HOW TSUNAMIS HAPPEN

This diagram shows how an earthquake on the seabed can cause a tsunami. The sudden movement causes a ripple in the water above it, making fast-moving waves spread out in all directions. In deep water, a tsunami wave is very long and shallow, and harmless to boats. But as it moves into shallow water near the coast, the wave slows down, and the water in it piles up, making it higher and more dangerous when it hits the land. And there's usually not just one wave, but a series of several in a row.

▼ *A huge tsunami hit Japan in March 2011. This photo shows the wave rushing ashore in the city of Natori.*

TSUNAMI SPEED

Before they reach land, tsunami waves travel very fast across the ocean surface. They can race along at 800 km/h (500 mph). That's the speed of a large passenger plane, and much faster than normal ocean waves. As the tsunami waves spread out across a sea or ocean, they get weaker. By the time they hit land, they've often slowed to the speed of a car. But a very big and powerful tsunami can travel a long way and still cause damage on faraway shores. Tsunami scientists use the speed of a tsunami to calculate how long it will take to reach different places. They can then send out tsunami warning alerts, so that people can escape to safety before the wave arrives.

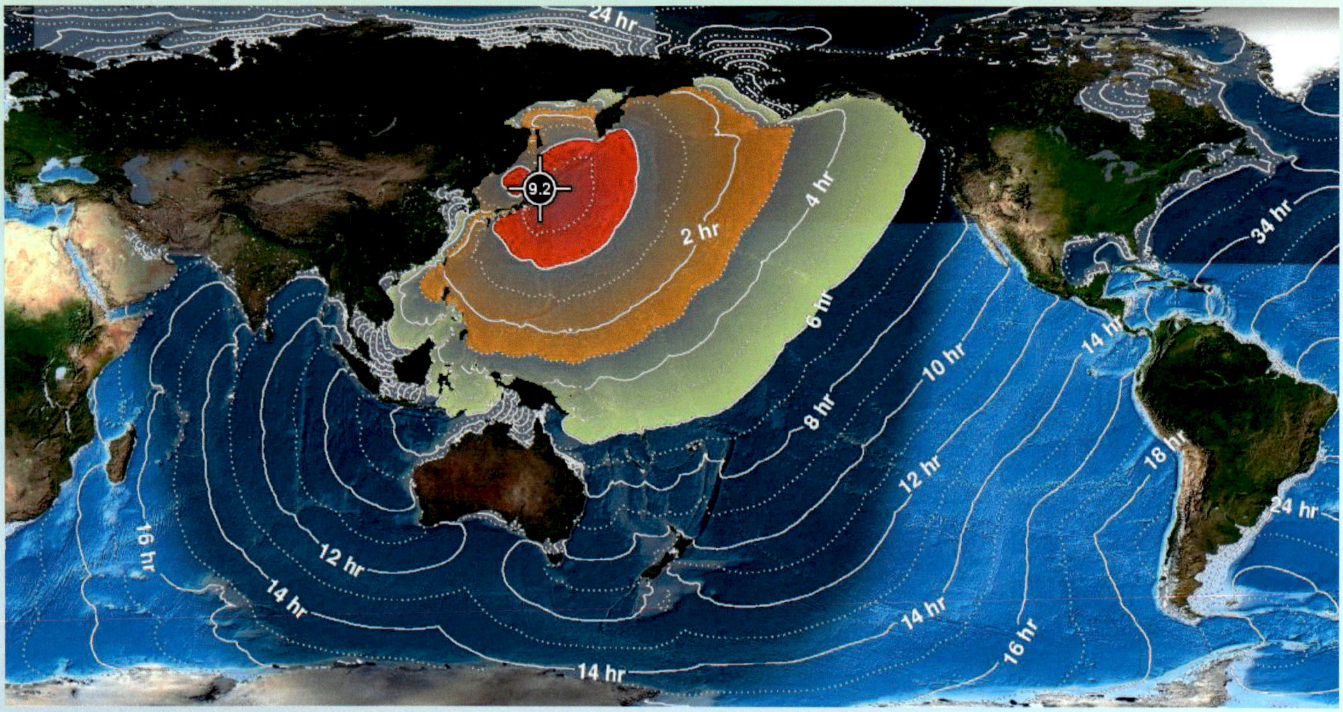

▲ *This map shows the travel times of a tsunami starting near Japan and spreading out across the Pacific Ocean. For example, it would take about eight hours to reach north Australia.*

HEADING FOR HIGHER GROUND

One of the best ways to stay safe when a tsunami is coming is to head uphill. That's because the water usually doesn't reach hilltops as it flows ashore and floods the land. In tsunami-prone areas, signs show people the best routes to take to reach high ground quickly. Strangely, many people have also noticed animals becoming stressed and moving uphill before a tsunami strikes. Scientists think some animals might be able to sense vibrations in the ground that we can't and know they are a sign of danger.

◀ *Farm animals, buffaloes, elephants, dogs and cats have all been seen moving to higher ground before a tsunami strikes.*

GLACIER TSUNAMI

A glacier is a slow-moving mass of ice in a mountain valley or covering a land mass, such as Antarctica. Some glaciers flow into the sea, and sometimes a big chunk breaks off, becoming an iceberg. The mass of ice falling into the sea can cause a tsunami. In some parts of the Arctic region, including Alaska and Greenland, moving or melting glaciers can also trigger landslides. When this happens, a mass of ice and rock plunge into the sea together. Events like this have caused several huge tsunamis.

▶ *In Greenland in 2023, a mountaintop (shown by the yellow line) and a mass of ice slid into the sea, causing a huge tsunami. The red line shows the height of the wave.*

▲ *An ice tsunami in Fort Erie, Canada, pushes onto the land past a row of trees, showing how high the ice pile is.*

ICE TSUNAMI

An ice tsunami, also called an 'ice shove', is much slower-moving than a water tsunami. It happens on the edge of a lake, or sometimes the sea, after the surface of the water has frozen into solid ice. When the weather gets warmer, usually in spring, the ice starts to break up into sections or chunks. Water currents or strong winds push the chunks of ice towards the land, where it piles up and pushes or tips over onto the shore. Though they are not usually as dangerous as a normal tsunami, ice tsunamis can damage docks, vehicles and houses, sometimes even crushing and destroying them completely.

VOLCANOES

A volcano is an opening in Earth's crust where hot, melted rock from under the ground can flow out, or erupt.

Most volcanoes are also mountains. As the lava (erupted rock) flows out of the ground, it cools and hardens. With each eruption, more rock builds up, forming a cone or dome shape. However, some volcanoes are just long, narrow cracks in the ground. Others are big underground chambers of magma (melted rock). When they erupt, the ground above the magma falls downward, forming a big bowl shape called a caldera.

HOW VOLCANOES WORK

A typical volcano has several parts. Below the volcano is the magma chamber, where hot, melted rock pushes up from. It rises up the conduit, a tube in the middle of the volcano, and erupts out of the vent, the opening at the top. Some volcanoes also have extra or secondary vents, and some have a crater at the top. The volcano itself is built up from layers of lava, ash or rock fragments, or

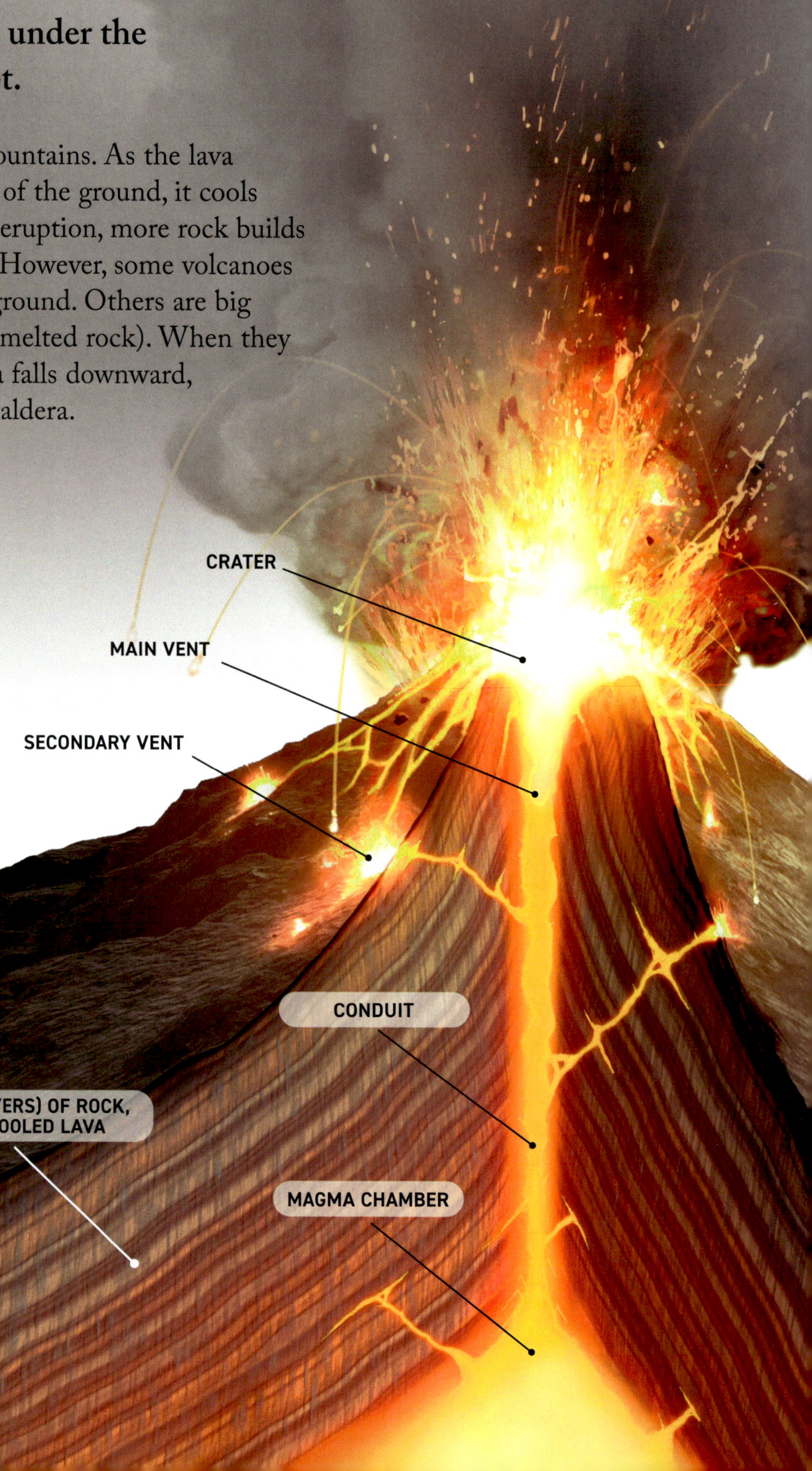

sometimes a combination. Like earthquakes, volcanoes are usually found around Earth's plate boundaries (see page 10). At divergent boundaries, where two plates pull away from each other, the crust thins and cracks, and magma rises up from below the crust to fill the gap. At convergent boundaries, where one plate pushes under another, the lower plate starts to melt, and magma moves upwards through cracks in the other plate. There are also 'hotspots' in Earth's crust, which can occur far away from plate boundaries. At a hotspot, a plume or standing column of extra-hot magma from deep inside the planet melts through the crust above it.

BUBBLING UNDER

This diagram shows a convergent plate boundary, where an oceanic (seabed) plate is pushing under a continental (land) plate. The seabed gradually moves deeper, carrying rocks with it that contain water. The trapped water makes the rocks around it melt more easily. This creates lots of hot, melted rock just under the crust. It rises upwards and forms volcanoes near the edge of the continental plate.

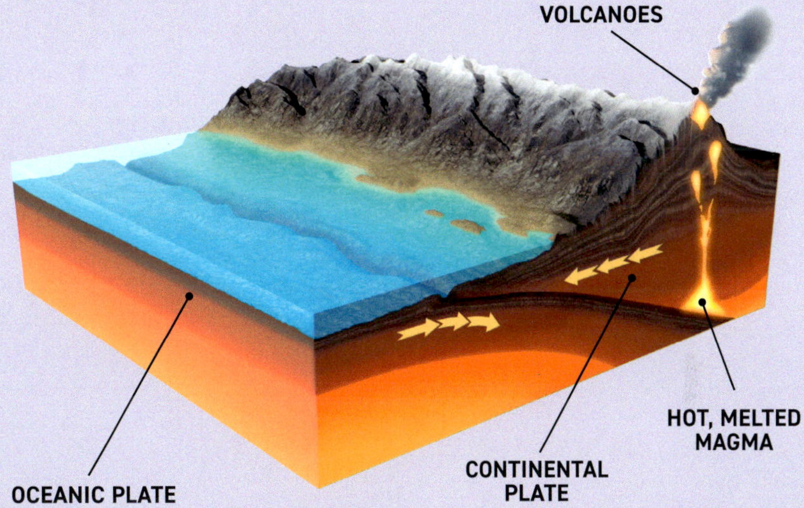

▶ *Some volcanoes release explosive gases that shatter magma and lava into tiny pieces, forming volcanic ash. Here, ash covers a house in the Canary Islands.*

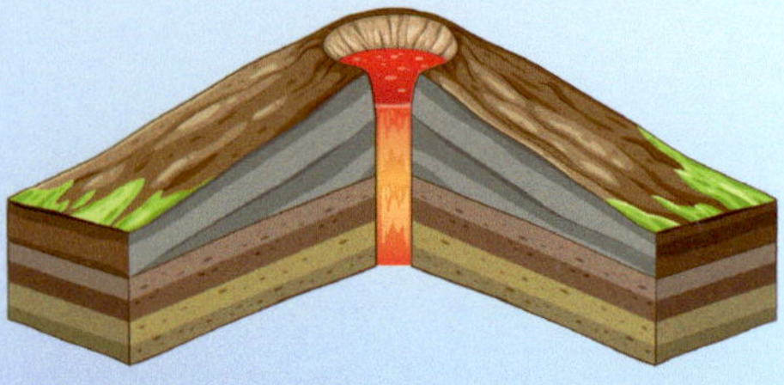

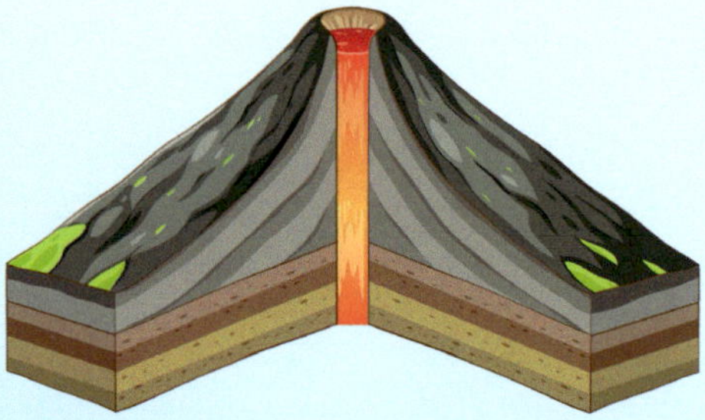

SHIELD VOLCANO

Shield volcanoes like Mauna Loa in Hawaii (below) are large, wide and flattish like a shield, with a rounded shape and gentle slopes. They form from very runny, liquid lava that flows a long way before cooling and hardening into solid rock. Over many eruptions, it builds up into a shield shape.

CINDER CONE VOLCANO

Cinder cones are usually quite small, and sometimes form on the sides of other volcanoes. They're made of tiny rock fragments, or cinders, that form when gases make magma explode as it erupts. The cinders pile up in a heap, forming a cone shape. The cinder cone pictured below is Mount Batok in Indonesia.

COMPOSITE VOLCANO

Stratovolcanoes have a tall, pointed cone shape. They have thick, gloopy lava that blocks the vent at the top of the volcano, so that pressure builds up inside. Then – BOOM! – an explosive eruption blasts out ash, rocks and lava. These different materials collect and build up in layers, forming the volcano's cone.

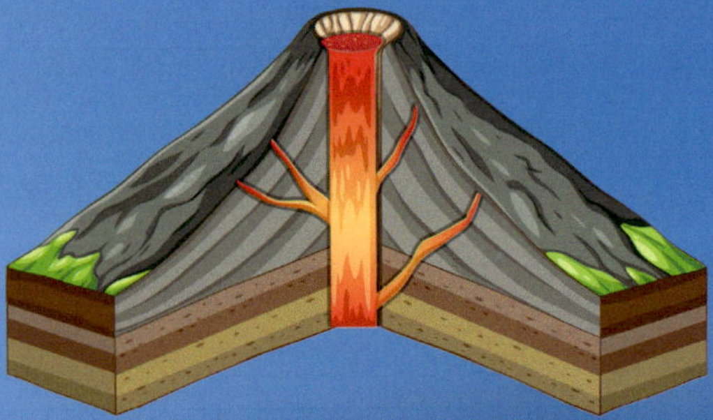

▶ *Mount Semeru is a stratovolcano on the island of Java in Indonesia. Though it erupts frequently, hikers often climb it.*

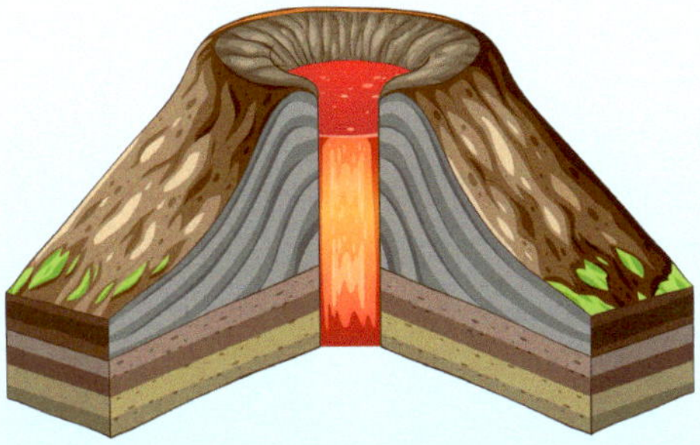

LAVA DOME VOLCANO

A lava dome is a rounded, dome-shaped volcano, formed by very slow-flowing, sticky lava. The lava is so thick that it cannot spread far before it cools and hardens. The Soufrière Hills volcano (below) is a famous example of a lava dome that buried the capital city on the Caribbean island of Montserrat.

FISSURE VOLCANO

A fissure volcano is a long crack or opening in the ground, where lava flows or explodes from underground. Fissures sometimes appear on or close to other types of volcanoes. They are also common in Iceland, where two plates are pulling apart, which can create cracks in the ground like those pictured here.

STUDYING VOLCANOES

The science of volcanoes is called volcanology. Volcanologists can study volcanoes from the air, or using data from satellites in orbit around Earth. They also get up close to active volcanoes to measure things like the temperature of lava and what chemicals it's made of, what types of gases are being released, and whether the ground is bulging or cracking. This can help to predict volcanic eruptions, but it is also very dangerous.

▶ *A volcanologist takes measurements during an eruption of Bárðarbunga, a stratovolcano in Iceland.*

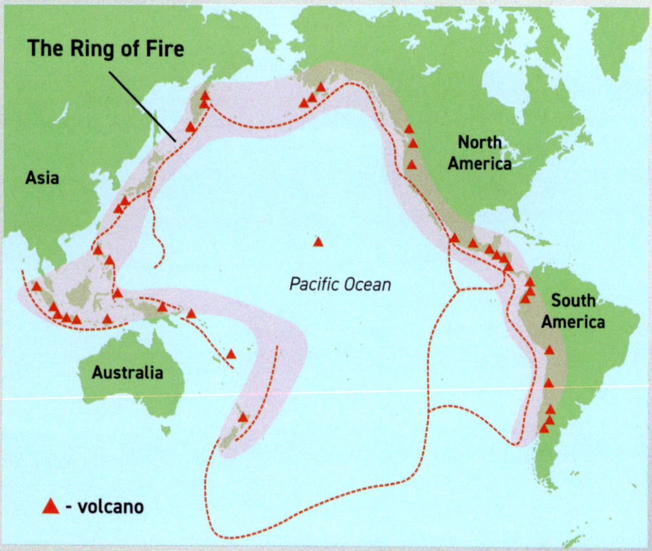

THE RING OF FIRE

Around the edges of the Pacific Ocean, the world's biggest ocean, are a series of plate boundaries. They cause frequent earthquakes and volcanoes, both on land and under the sea. As there are so many volcanic eruptions here, it is known as the 'Ring of Fire'. In total, the chain of volcanoes and volcanic activity is about 40,000 km (25,000 miles) long, with more than 450 volcanoes dotted along it.

◀ *The Ring of Fire runs through several of the world's most volcanic countries, including Indonesia, Japan, the USA and Chile.*

PEOPLE OF POMPEII

One of the most famous volcanic eruptions in history took place in what is now Italy in 79 CE. The stratovolcano Vesuvius erupted violently, covering the town of Pompeii in hot volcanic ash, gas and rock fragments. Many people were buried by the ash, which hardened, leaving body-shaped hollows. Some of these have been used to make casts like this one.

VOLCANIC LIGHTNING

During a big eruption, a tall cloud or 'plume' of ash and gases can form above a volcano. Sometimes, lightning appears inside the plume. In a normal thunderstorm, electric charge builds up when ice particles crash together inside clouds. The same thing can happen in a volcanic plume, but with ash and rock particles. When enough electrical charge has collected, it is released as a lightning bolt. This is sometimes called a 'dirty thunderstorm'.

▼ *The Russian volcano Tolbachik erupts. Located on the remote eastern Kamchatka Peninsula, it is part of the Ring of Fire.*

ACTIVE, DORMANT OR EXTINCT?

Volcanoes can be classified as active, dormant or extinct. An active volcano has erupted recently – in earth science, that means in the last 10,000 years or so. A dormant (meaning 'sleeping') volcano is not active but could erupt again, and an extinct volcano is one that scientists think has completely stopped erupting. It can, however, be hard to tell if a volcano really is extinct.

MOUNT ETNA

Towering over the Italian island of Sicily, Mount Etna is Europe's tallest and most active volcano. The earliest human records of it erupting date back to 1500 BCE, and it has been erupting regularly since, including dozens of times in the 21st century. The summit of the stratovolcano has multiple craters and vents that are constantly emitting gas and steam.

LANDSLIDES AND MUDFLOWS

Landslides and mudflows happen when a large amount of mud, rock or soil suddenly slips, falls or flows downhill.

Earth scientists call these events 'mass movement'. As you can imagine, a landslide, a river of mud or a mass of rock falling from a cliff can cause a deadly disaster if there are people in the way. They can flatten houses – or sometimes whole towns – and damage roads and bridges. Sometimes, they cause other disasters, too. For example, a big landslide falling into water can set off a tsunami.

HOW IT HAPPENS

All landslides, rockfalls and mudflows are pulled downwards by gravity, but they can be triggered in several ways. Sometimes, an earthquake or volcanic eruption shakes the land so much that a section separates and slides downhill. Landslides can also happen when a rainstorm soaks the soil or rock on a hillside, making it waterlogged and heavy.

A lahar is a volcanic mudflow,

▼ *These houses were destroyed by a lahar flowing down Mount Merapi in Indonesia, after a big eruption in 2010 was followed by heavy rain.*

created when ash, dust or rocks from a volcanic eruption mix with water from heavy rain or melting snow to make a river of thick mud.

A cliff fall happens when part of a cliff suddenly crumbles or splits off and collapses in a heap. This is especially common on the coast, where crashing waves constantly wear away at the rocks, and every so often, a chunk falls off.

▲ *Cliff falls are common on the southern coast of England. Heavy rains drench the top of the cliff, making it heavy and more likely to slide off.*

RESCUE EFFORTS

After a landslide or mudslide, rescue teams have to work fast to find and pull out any survivors stuck under the mud, soil or rock. As in earthquake rescues, they use sniffer dogs to help find people, along with diggers and bulldozers to carefully clear the debris away from homes and vehicles. Sometimes, people survive inside houses or cars that have been buried, and can be pulled out to safety. But rescue efforts can be dangerous for the rescuers, too, as it's easy to get stuck in the mud themselves.

◀ *Rescuers search for survivors in wet mud and soil after a landslide struck the Oso area, in Washington state, USA, in 2014.*

TYPES OF FALLS AND SLIDES

Scientists sort landslides, mudflows and other mass movements into four main types, depending on the way the material moves as gravity pulls it down.

FALLS

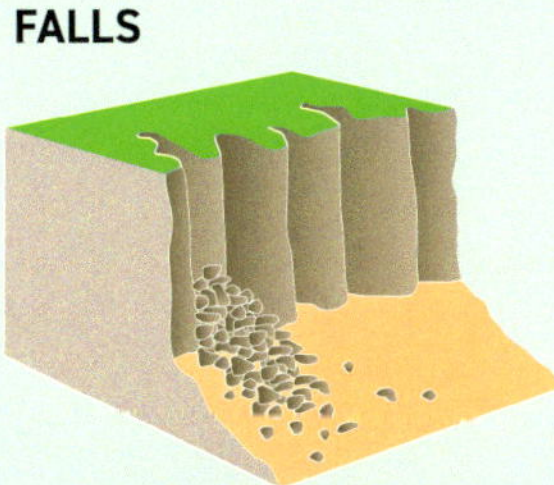

▲ *Falls happen when rock or soil moves down a very steep slope or vertical cliff face, piling up at the bottom.*

TOPPLES

▲ *In a topple, a solid material, such as rock, leans forwards and tips over, before crashing violently to the ground.*

SLIDES

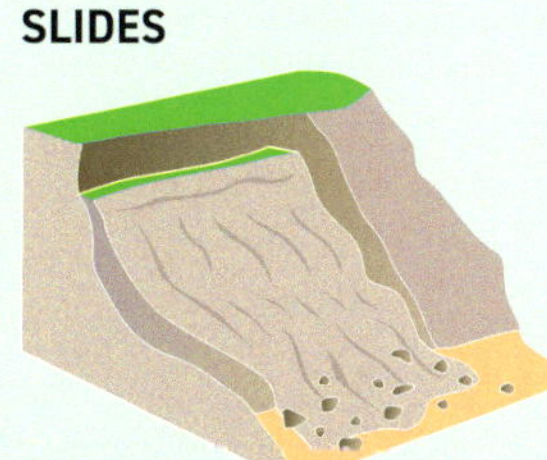

▲ *A slide happens when a large section of land separates from the rock or soil beneath it and slips downhill.*

FLOWS

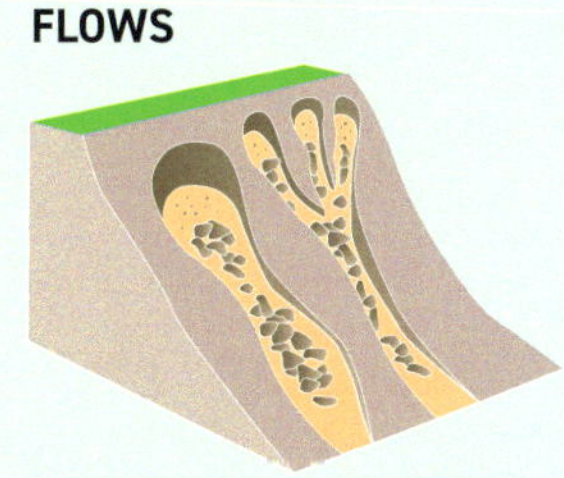

▲ *A flow works like a moving river of liquid, running downhill in channels. Flows can be made of mud, soil or loose rocks.*

SINKHOLES

A sinkhole is just what it sounds like! The ground sinks downwards, creating a hole. They range from small dimples to huge caverns.

The idea of a hole suddenly opening up in the ground is pretty scary, but don't panic! While sinkholes can be dangerous, big ones are quite rare, and they don't happen everywhere. They are most likely in places where the rocks underground are easily dissolved by water. Gradually, caves and holes can open up underground, and that's what causes a sinkhole. Sometimes, human activities can cause sinkholes, too.

▶ *This parked car fell into a sinkhole that appeared in London, England, in 2016 – but luckily no one was injured.*

HOW IT WORKS

Most sinkholes are caused by water flowing underground. In some types of rock, such as limestone, chalk and gypsum, water moving below the surface gradually dissolves the rock, forming tunnels and caves. If a cave or gap is close to the surface, the soil and rocks above can fall down into it, making a sinkhole. Sometimes, leaks from water pipes wash away underground sand or loose rocks, creating a human-made sinkhole. This type of sinkhole is more common in cities. Big, deep sinkholes can cause disasters if they swallow up people or buildings.

SINKHOLE UNDER THE SEA

There are sinkholes underwater, too, like the famous Great Blue Hole, near Belize in Central America. It began as an underground cave, thousands of years ago when the sea level was much lower than it is today. As the sea rose and covered it, the cave roof collapsed, forming one of the biggest sinkholes in the world. It's almost a perfect circle, which is about 318 m (1,043 ft) across and reaches 124 m (406 ft) deep, surrounded by shallower water. Today, the distinctive sinkhole is a tourist attraction and a popular destination for SCUBA divers.

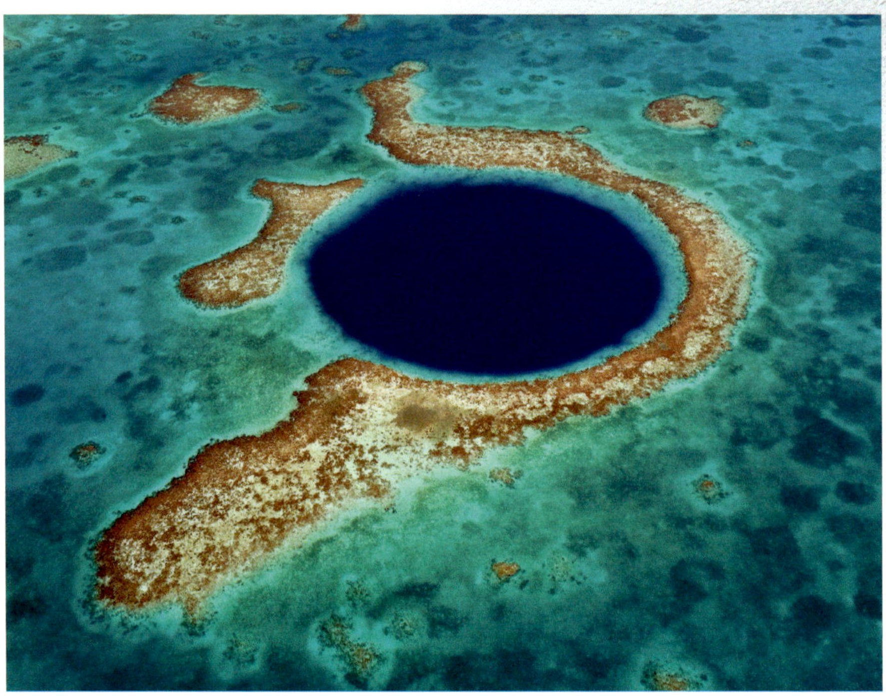

▲ *The Great Blue Hole in the Caribbean Sea near Belize, seen from the air.*

SINKHOLE SEQUENCE

This diagram shows how sinkholes can form in landscapes made of limestone rock, also known as karst landscapes. They often have a layer of limestone bedrock, or solid rock, with a covering of looser rocks, clay and soil on top. Some sinkholes can open up suddenly and dramatically, but the processes that lead to them forming can sometimes take hundreds or even thousands of years.

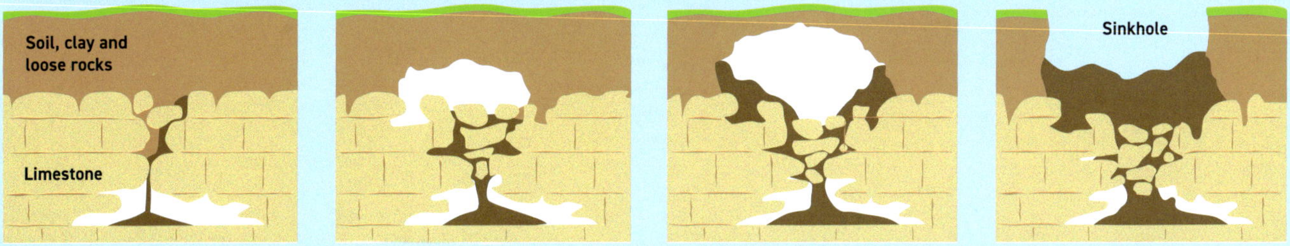

▲ *Water soaking and flowing through underground limestone forms cracks and caverns as it slowly dissolves and washes away the rock.*

▲ *As holes form, the soil and rock above can fall down into them, creating a hole nearer to the surface.*

▲ *As more rocks and soil slip downwards, they leave only a thin layer of surface ground covering the hole.*

▲ *The sinkhole appears when the thin surface soil and rock layer suddenly gives way and collapses into the gap below.*

PYROCLASTIC FLOWS

When a volcano erupts or a lava dome collapses, it can trigger an avalanche of super-hot gas, ash, and fragmented rock that plummets down slopes at incredible speeds. Known as pyroclastic flows, these deadly volcanic hazards can reach temperatures above 800°C (1500°F) and move at speeds of more than 100 km/h (60 mph), burning up and flattening everything in their paths.

METEORITE IMPACTS

A meteorite is a piece of rock or metal from space that gets pulled in by Earth's gravity and crashes into it.

Meteorites usually come from asteroids or comets – small space objects that orbit the Sun – but any fragment of space rock can become a meteorite. As a piece of rock falls through Earth's atmosphere, it heats up and most often burns away to nothing. It may be visible as a streak of light in the night sky, called a meteor or shooting star. Those that land on the ground, however, are called meteorites.

METEORITE IMPACTS

Thousands of meteorites impact Earth every year. Most are smaller than a tennis ball and go unnoticed as they land in remote areas or in the sea. Very occasionally, they land on a house, and in 1954, one hit a woman in the US state of Alabama (she survived). But large meteorites are extremely rare. We know they have crashed into Earth in the past because they have left large, bowl-shaped impact craters that mark where they hit.

DON'T WORRY!

Big meteorite impacts can cause major disasters. A meteorite that is 200 m (650 ft) wide could level a city. One that is 2 km (1 mile) or more can affect the whole planet, with massive shock waves. They can ignite wildfires and trigger earthquakes, volcanic eruptions, and tsunamis. They can also fill the sky with dust and ash, blocking out sunlight and killing off the plants that are the base of our food chains. This global cloud could change the climate overnight and take years to settle.

However, we now have powerful telescopes and monitoring systems that help us to spot space objects coming towards Earth long before they arrive. If an asteroid or comet was on a collision course with us, we might be able to send a rocket to crash into it and push it in a different direction.

▼ *Meteor Crater, in Arizona, USA, was made by a meteorite about 50 m (160 ft) across that landed about 50,000 years ago.*

▲ *This map shows where large meteorites, bigger than 10 km (6 miles) across, have left craters around the world.*

DINOSAUR DISASTER

About 66 million years ago, a huge asteroid impact ended the Age of the Dinosaurs. It caused tsunamis, wildfires, and dark skies that killed off plants and led to many species dying out entirely. We've found evidence of the crater it left off the coast of Mexico and calculated it was around 10 km (6 miles) across, leaving a 200-km (120-mile) crater.

THE TUNGUSKA METEOR

In June 1908, a large asteroid came zooming towards Earth over the forested Tunguska-River area of Siberia, Russia. However, instead of landing and becoming a meteorite, it grew so hot that it exploded in mid-air, about 7 km (4 miles) above the ground. Only a few people saw it, as the area is so remote, but the huge, fiery blast flattened millions of trees. Scientists have estimated the asteroid was about 50-60 m (165-200 ft) wide.

EXTREME EVENTS

Around the world, dozens of major geological events and natural disasters make their way into the news headlines every year.

These extreme geological events are a selection of some the most dangerous and record-breaking examples in recent history – such as the strongest earthquake, the most destructive volcanic eruption, the deadliest tsunami and the most disastrous landslide. The map below shows where each one happened.

Earthquake
Valdivia, Chile, 1960

On 22 May 1960, the strongest earthquake on record struck near Valdivia in Chile, South America. It measured about M9.5 on the moment magnitude scale (see page 15). Although almost 2,000 people died, the death toll was lower than that of many other earthquakes, as tremors had warned people it was coming.

Tsunami
Indian Ocean, 2004

In late December 2004, a huge M9.1 earthquake on the seabed near Indonesia triggered massive tsunami waves. They spread out across the Indian Ocean, causing widespread destruction on the coasts of surrounding countries and killing almost 230,000 people.

Landslide
Vargas, Venzuela, 1999

A powerful rainstorm hit Venezuela, South America, in December 1999. It soaked the soil on the steep mountains along the coast, leading to the worst ever landslide disaster in history. Multiple landslides and mudflows washed away homes and buried coastal towns.

Volcano
Mount St Helens, USA, 1980

In May 1980, the stratovolcano Mount St Helens in Washington state, USA, blew up in an enormous explosive eruption. It wasn't the deadliest eruption on record, as most people in the area had been evacuated, but it did feature the biggest landslide in history, as the whole top of the mountain collapsed.

Sinkhole
Guatemala City, 2010

This famous sinkhole opened up in the ground in Guatemala City, Guatemala, Central America, in 2010. It was 18 m (60 ft) wide and 100 m (330 ft) deep, and was caused by underground water leaks washing away the loose volcanic gravel that part of the city is built on. The hole swallowed up an intersection and a factory.

Meteorite impact
Chelyabinsk, Russia, 2013

Early on 15 February 2013, people in Chelyabinsk, Russia, saw a meteor zoom across the sky. It was an asteroid bigger than a house, moving at 69,000 km/h (42,690 mph) – but before reaching the ground, it exploded into pieces. Though not deadly, the sudden blast shattered windows in thousands of nearby homes.

2 EXTREME HEAT

HOW THE SUN WORKS

The star in the middle of our Solar System, the Sun gives off vast amounts of heat and light, making life on Earth possible.

All life on Earth depends on the Sun. Gravity – the force that attracts objects in space towards each other – keeps Earth orbiting around it. Our planet is 150 million km (93 million miles) from the Sun. It's just the right distance to make Earth warm enough for life. Sunlight allows plants to grow, which in turn support the rest of the food chain.

HEAT AND LIGHT

The Sun is a giant ball of gas. It is mostly made of hydrogen and helium. It releases vast amounts of energy. The core at the centre is the hottest part, reaching about 15,600,000°C (about 28,080,000°F). The surface is much cooler – 'only' 6,000°C (about 10,000°F). Darker, cooler patches called sunspots sometimes appear on the surface. Around the Sun, layers of gases form its atmosphere. The corona is the outer atmosphere, which reaches 2,000,000°C (3,600,000°F).

In the core, the hydrogen atoms are packed in very tightly. Great heat and pressure squeeze the hydrogen. The atoms collide and stick together – this is called nuclear fusion. It creates a heavier atom – helium. The process of nuclear fusion releases a huge amount of energy as heat and light. Every second, the Sun turns more than 600 million tonnes (590 million tons) of hydrogen into helium. The energy travels from the core to the Sun's surface, which takes about 170,000 years. From the surface, the solar radiation – heat and light energy – takes just eight minutes to travel to Earth.

HOW THE SUN HEATS EARTH

The Equator faces the Sun all year round. The Sun's rays strike Earth directly over a small area, so the Equator receives lots of heat. At the poles, it is dark for six months every year. When they face the Sun, the rays strike at a slanted angle and spread over a large area, so the poles receive little heat.

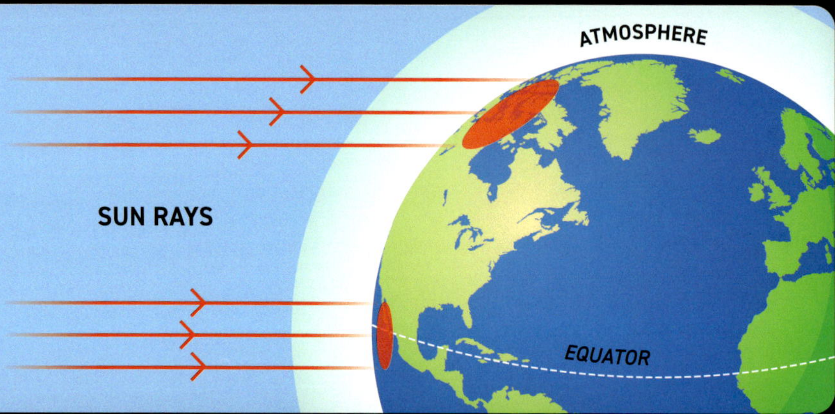

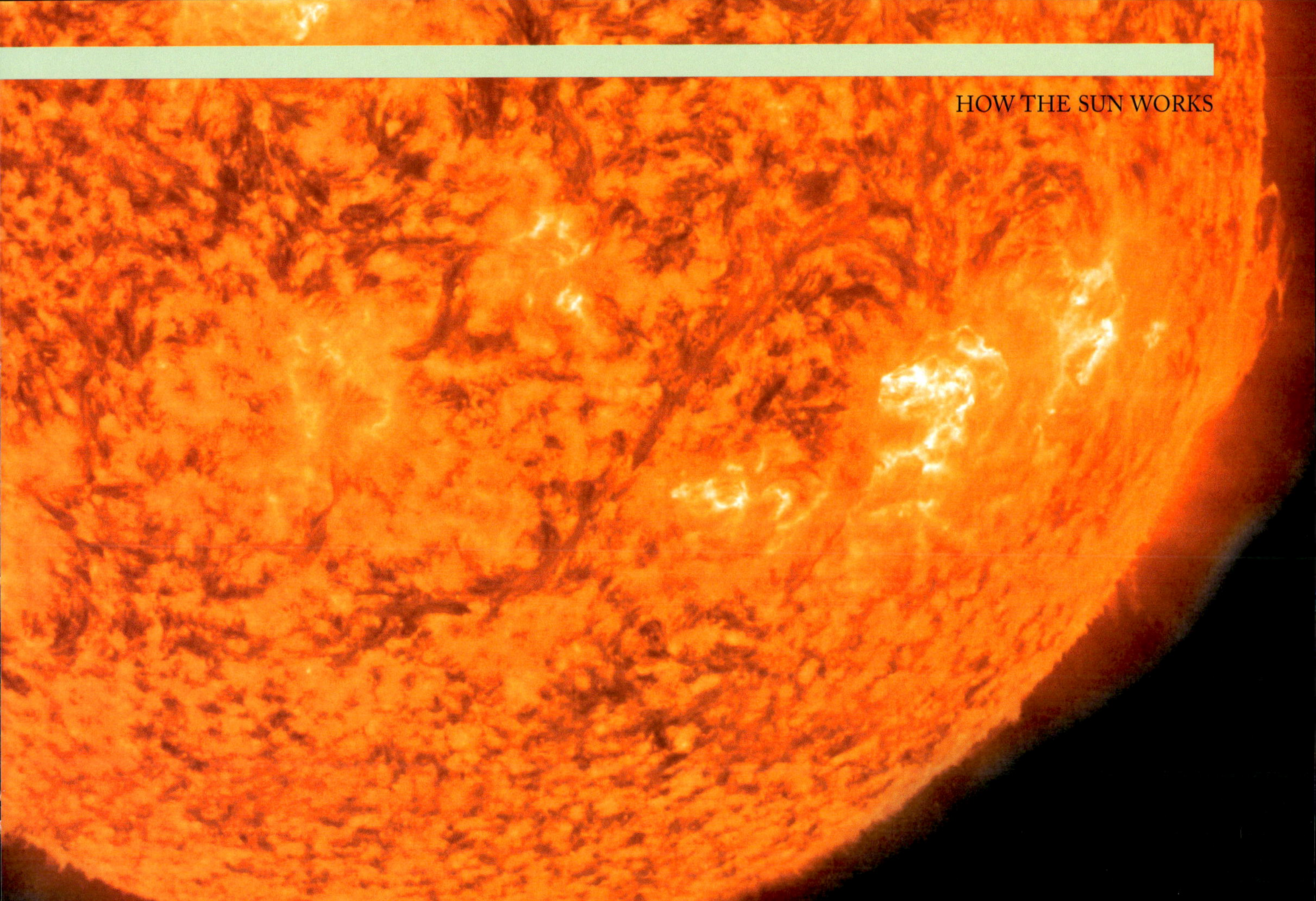

▲ *The Sun, photographed with a special light. The bright spots are active regions, including solar flares releasing intense light and radiation.*

SOLAR RADIATION

Energy from the Sun includes visible radiation, which we see as light, and invisible radiation, such as radio waves and microwaves.

INFRARED Humans cannot see it, but they detect it as heat.

LIGHT We see sunlight as white light.

ULTRAVIOLET (UV) UV waves carry more energy than visible light. They can burn you, which is why it's crucial to use suncream.

X-RAYS These come from the Sun's corona and have more energy than UV rays. They can pass through substances that light cannot, such as people's bodies.

▲ *Invented in 1853 and still used today, the Campbell-Stokes sunshine recorder measures and records the number of sunlight hours, providing long-term data for scientists.*

HEATWAVES

During a heatwave, the days and nights are unusually hot for the local area. A heatwave can last from a few days to months.

Heatwaves usually happen in the summer when there are high-pressure weather systems – periods of dry, settled weather with no rain. High-pressure systems force cool, dense air to sink, and it warms as it falls towards the ground. They trap the hot air there, stopping it from rising and cooling to form clouds, so the skies are clear and sunny. High-pressure systems can last for days or for many weeks.

IMPACTS OF HEATWAVES

Heatwaves are one of the most dangerous natural weather events. High temperatures at night are an even greater problem than soaring daytime temperatures. If it is unusually hot at night, the temperature rises more quickly during the day, and high temperatures last for longer. It is harder for people and wildlife to recover from the heat if they cannot rest well at night.

The very young, the very elderly and people with health problems are affected the worst because it is harder for their bodies to stay at a normal temperature. They may get rashes, cramps, exhaustion or even collapse with heatstroke, which is a life-threatening condition that occurs when the body overheats.

Extreme heat makes it hard for people to continue daily life. Schools are often closed.

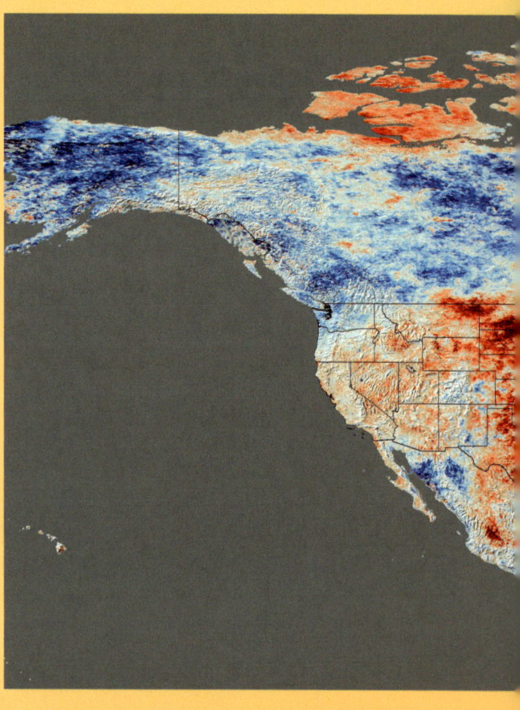

▲ *This map shows the increased temperatures during a heatwave in the Northern Hemisphere in the summer of 2006. The red areas show higher temperatures compared to the averages for that period over the previous six years.*

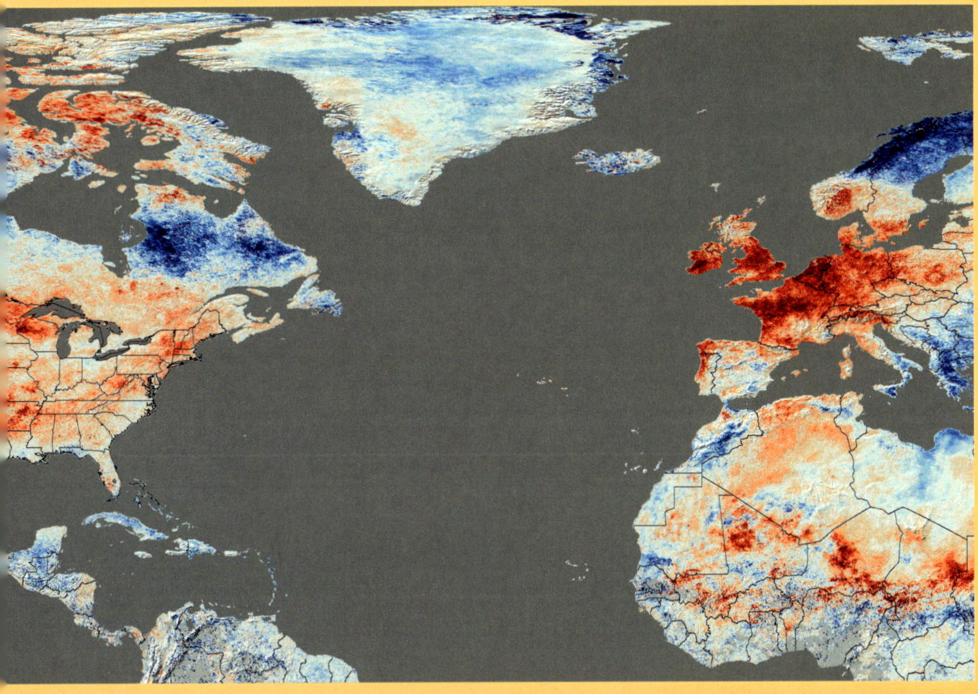

Outdoor workers struggle to do their jobs. The heat puts a strain on services and the economy. For example, people use more water to keep cool and more electricity for air-conditioning. On farms, crops may be damaged by the heat, and animals may suffer or die.

CLIMATE CHANGE

Most scientists agree that heatwaves are becoming more common and severe owing to climate change. Carbon dioxide is building up in Earth's atmosphere because of human activities such as burning oil, coal and gas. The carbon dioxide traps in heat, making temperatures on Earth rise. This is global warming (see page 48). In February 2025, several regions of East Africa experienced extreme heat linked to climate change. Heatwaves across Europe that summer caused 16,500 extra deaths.

HOW TO KEEP COOL

During a heatwave, drink lots of water and exercise at a cool time of the day. If you need to go out, stay in the shade and take water with you. Check on elderly people, those who are unwell and families with young babies. If you have pets, make sure they keep out of the sun and drink plenty of water.

GREENHOUSE EFFECT

The warming of the Earth's surface and atmosphere is called the Greenhouse Effect. It is caused by gases in the air that trap the Sun's energy.

The gases in the atmosphere that trap heat are called greenhouse gases. They work like greenhouse glass, allowing energy to reach Earth's surface and stopping it from escaping. Without greenhouse gases, it would be too cold for life on Earth – the average temperature would be around that of a home freezer. When levels of greenhouse gas get too high, it can lead to dangerous climate changes.

HOW IT LEADS TO GLOBAL WARMING

Heat energy radiates from the Sun, and some of it reaches Earth. Some of the heat energy is absorbed, and some is reflected off the atmosphere or off pale, shiny surfaces like ice and escapes back into space (yellow arrows). The greenhouse gases in the atmosphere trap escaping heat energy, so that some of it returns to Earth's surface and lower atmosphere and warms it up (orange arrow).

GLOBAL WARMING

For most of human history, the temperature of Earth changed slowly, in a cycle between ice ages and warmer periods when temperatures were higher than now. These changes took hundreds of thousands of years. Since the Industrial Revolution (1750–1900), Earth has warmed much faster than ever before.

The Industrial Revolution started in Europe and spread across the world from the 19th century. People used fossil fuels (coal, oil and gas) to power factories, buildings and transport. Burning fossil fuels gives off huge amounts of the greenhouse gas carbon dioxide. Between 1970 and 2004 alone, the quantity of greenhouse gases given off increased by 70 per cent.

Most scientists agree that the rapid rise in greenhouse gases is due to human activities. Earth's temperature has risen on average by 0.06 °C (0.11 °F) per decade since 1850. Since 1975, it has increased by 0.2 °C (0.36 °F) per decade. It could increase by 1.8 °C–4 °C (3.2 °F–7.2 °F) above pre-industrial levels by 2100.

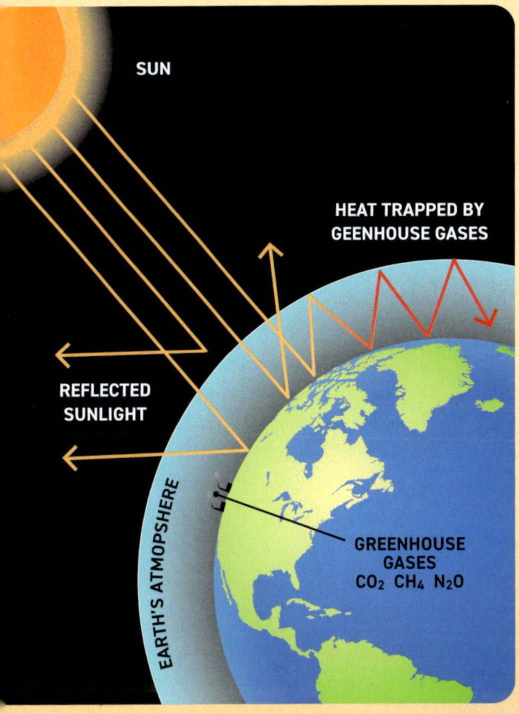

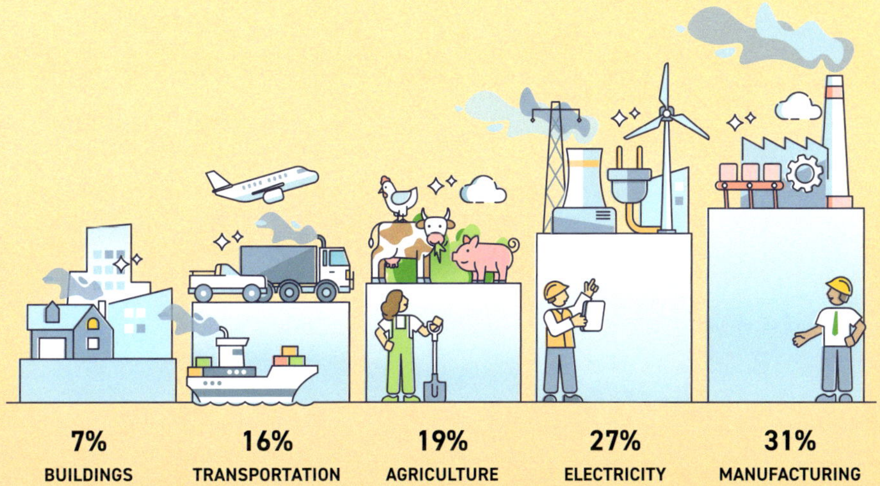

WHAT CREATES GREENHOUSE GASES?

Water vapour (created when water heats and turns to a gas), carbon dioxide and methane are the most common greenhouse gases. Before the Industrial Revolution, greenhouse gas levels had been fairly stable for thousands of years. Human activities have increased all of them except for water vapour. Most carbon dioxide (CO_2) comes from burning fossil fuels in factories, power plants and buildings, and in cars, planes, trucks and trains. Cutting down forests, burning wood and stopping CO_2-absorbing trees from growing back also leads to a net increase in carbon in the air. Methane mostly comes from farm animals (through burping and farting), from leaks and venting gas at oil fields, and from landfill sites.

▼ *Factories that burn fossil fuels pump out carbon dioxide into the atmosphere.*

CLIMATE ZONES

Climate is the pattern of weather over a long time. The main climate zones are polar, temperate and tropical.

The polar zones in the Arctic and Antarctic (blue on the map) are extremely cold even in summer. The temperate climate zones (green)have milder temperatures and the subtropical zones (yellow) are warmer still. Both usually have four seasons, and it is hot in summer and cooler in winter. In tropical climates around the Equator (red), it is very warm all year round, with a wet season and a dry season. Owing to human activities, climates worldwide are changing, making natural disasters more severe.

▸ Rapid warming of the Arctic climate leads to melting of the summer sea ice. Animals that depend on it to hunt are at great risk.

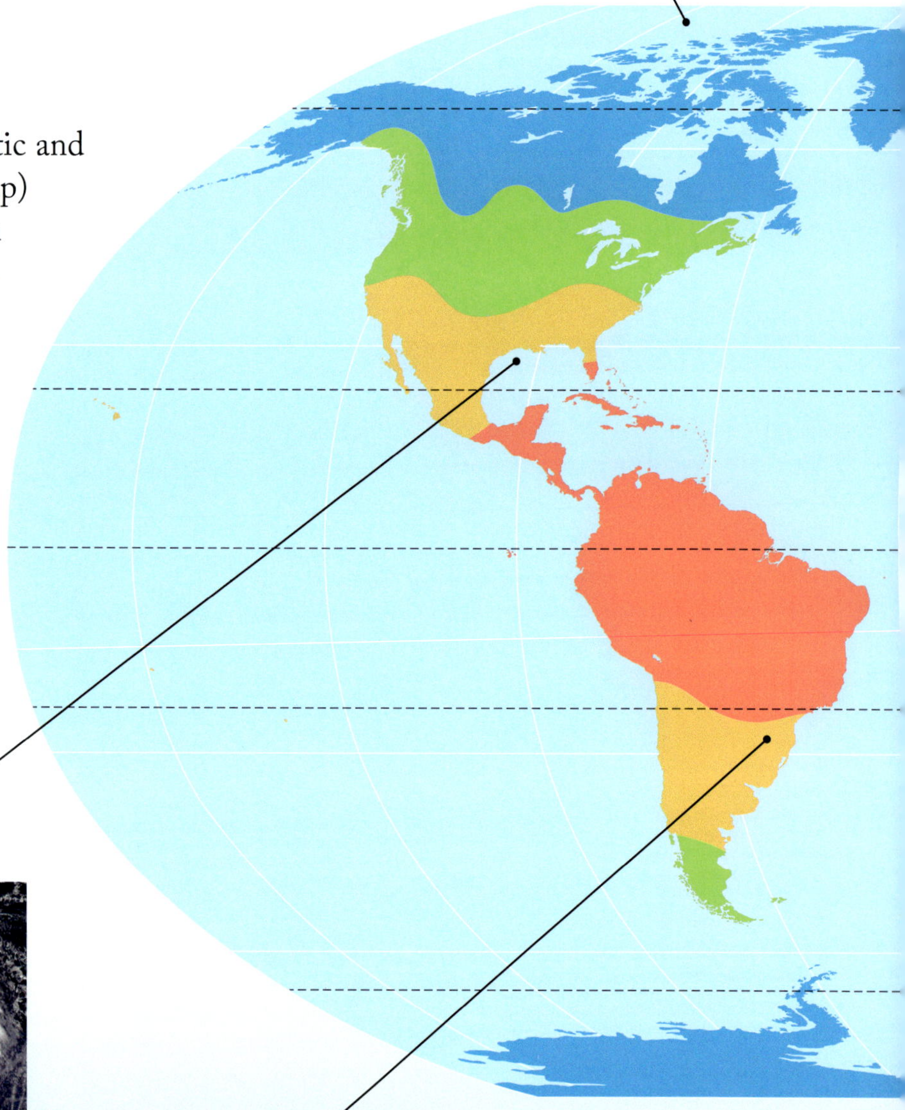

▴ Although it is not thought that climate change makes hurricanes in tropical North America more frequent, warmer oceans and atmosphere can make them more intense.

◂ In the tropical region of Rio Grande do Sul, Brazil, heavy rains flooded nearly every city in 2024 – the worst flood yet in southern Brazil.

◀ *Extreme heat causes more frequent and intense wildfires even in temperate zones. In 2025, Europe had the worst wildfire season since records began in 2006.*

◀ *Flooding is a normal feature of the rainy season in the tropical monsoon regions of Bangladesh. Climate change is making the floods much heavier though.*

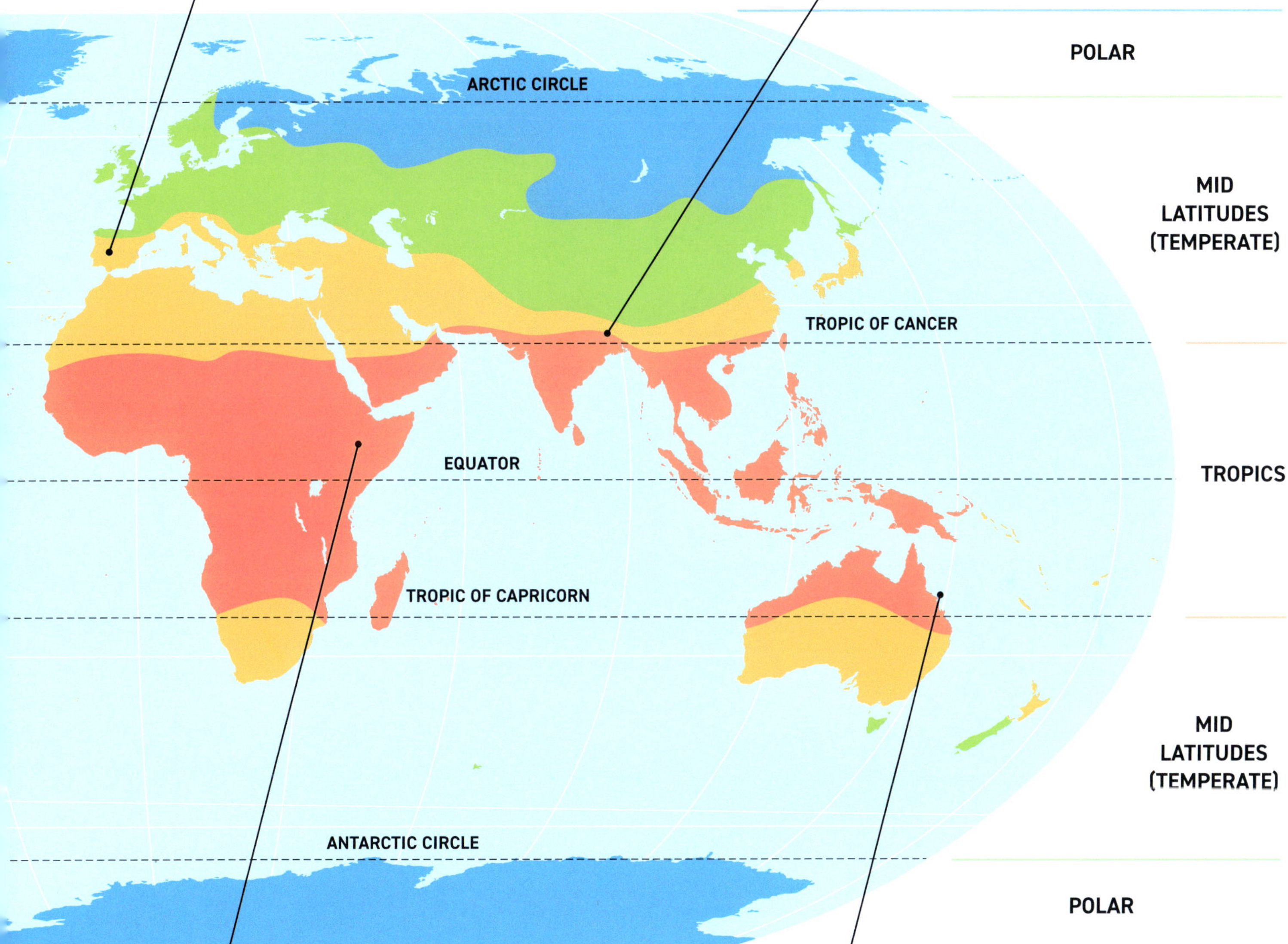

◀ *Over two years of low rainfall and high temperatures from 2023 caused drought across different climate zones of northern, southern and central-western Africa, destroying crops.*

◀ *In the tropical Great Barrier Reef, Australia, heat stress from rising ocean temperatures bleaches the coral, making it transparent. It is not dead but weakened.*

MELTING ICE AND RAPID WARMING

Located in the far northern islands of Svalbard, Norway's Austfonna ice cap is the third largest in the world, but it is melting at a rapid rate. Powerful waterfalls can be seen cascading from its edges as the ice continues to thin, contributing to sea-level rise. When ice (which reflects light) melts, more heat energy is absorbed by the dark seawater that is exposed, leading to more warming and melting. It's a vicious cycle that means the Arctic is warming four times faster than the global average.

DROUGHTS

When a place has less rain or snowfall than normal for a long time, a drought occurs. Droughts leave people without water for farming and daily life.

Some droughts are caused by changes in the winds that usually bring rain. Others are caused by changing ocean currents, which affect the amount of moisture in the air and the temperature. With global warming, some areas are growing hotter and have less rainfall. Human activities can make droughts more severe. Using lots of water to irrigate crops reduces the water in rivers, lakes and groundwater (water from under the ground). Cutting down trees reduces the water held in the soil as the water flows off the surface, leaving it dry.

EFFECTS OF DROUGHT

When there is not enough rain, farmers need to use water from rivers, lakes, streams or wells for their crops. If there is not enough, people – usually women and children – must travel further to find water for drinking, washing and cooking. If the sources of water run low, people cannot irrigate their crops. The crops may die, and livestock may die, too, so farmers lose their income. With less food being grown and high demand, the prices go up.

Drought can cause long-term problems. The lack of rainfall can lead to soil erosion – the topsoil (top layer of soil) blows away, making it less fertile (good for growing crops). The soil can become hard and cracked. Severe droughts can continue for months or even years. People can be forced to leave their homes and farms to move to areas with more water, or to a city to seek other work.

▼ *When mud dries, it takes up less space than wet mud, so cracks appear between lumps of earth.*

HISTORIC DROUGHTS

Scientists study historical droughts because learning about past weather patterns helps them to understand modern droughts. They examine tree rings, which show how much a tree grew in a particular year. In dry or drought years, the rings will be thinner because the tree grew less.

◀ *The Dust Bowl (1930s) was the worst drought in US history. Farmland turned to dust and winds blew the soil away so crops could not grow.*

TREE RINGS

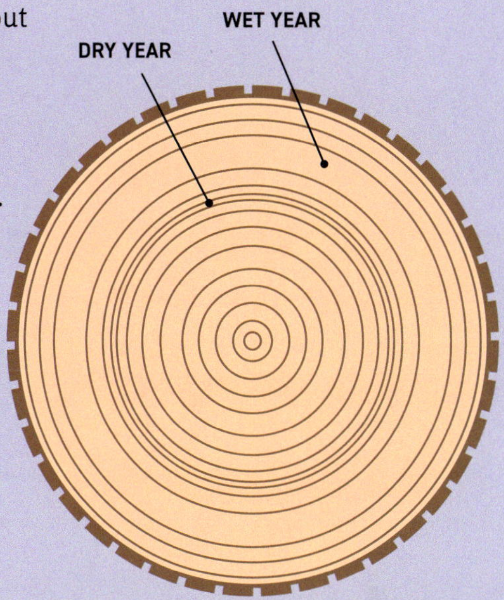

▶ *People fill their water sacks with groundwater from a well in the desert in Sudan.*

WILDFIRES

Out-of-control fires that spread through vegetation, wildfires can reach extreme heights and speeds and burn everything in their paths.

For a fire to break out, three ingredients are needed: heat, oxygen and fuel. Oxygen is in the air. In the wilderness, fuel comes from trees and plants. Heat can come from an open flame, power lines pulled down by a storm, or lightning. Once a wildfire takes hold, it can spread quickly if the weather is windy and the fuel is dry. It jumps easily from trees and plants to buildings and homes, harming people, animals and forests.

BENEFITS OF FIRE

Wildfires kill diseased trees, dead branches and grasses, returning nutrients to the soil (substances needed to keep living things alive and help them to grow). Fires burn through the dense forest canopy, the highest layer of branches, allowing sunlight to reach the forest floor so new plants can grow. Some kinds of pine cones need fire to release their seeds.

HAZARDS

Because of climate change, wildfires are happening more often, last longer and are more severe. The combination of heatwaves, droughts and high winds – which are all occurring more frequently – allows wildfires to start more easily. Heatwaves cause higher temperatures. Droughts dry out trees and plants, so they catch fire more readily. Strong winds spread fires faster. Higher temperatures melt winter snow earlier, so the land is drier for a longer time. In 2024, forest fires burnt twice as much tree cover than they did 20 years earlier – losing an amount of forest about the same size as Greece.

AREAS AT MOST RISK

More than half the land burnt by wildfires each year is on the hottest continent, Africa, in its grasslands, savannahs and shrublands. However, around 60 per cent of forest fires from 2001–24 broke out in boreal forests: cold, northern forests in countries including Russia, China, Canada and the USA, where nearly 85 per cent of wildfires are caused by humans. These regions are warming at a faster rate than most of the rest of the Earth. Naturally dry areas such as the Western USA are also at great risk. Despite high rainfall, wildfire damage is increasing in the tropical forests of South America and the Congo Basin because of deforestation (cutting down trees) and drought.

▼ *A wildfire destroys a pine forest in the Canary Islands in southern Europe. Wildfires occur naturally here but have grown worse.*

▲ *Flames burn sage brush plants in Idaho, north-western USA, a dry region that experiences immense and severe fires.*

TYPES OF FOREST FIRE

Ground fires begin on the forest floor, burning roots, dried leaves and other buried plant matter. As there is little oxygen, the fire grows slowly, making lots of smoke. Surface fires burn trees, bushes and grass, and they travel faster. Crown fires are the most dangerous and develop fastest of all. The wind spreads them through the canopy, and the flames can leap from treetop to treetop.

HUMAN CAUSES

More than 1.6 billion people live within 5 km (3 miles) of a forest. In tropical areas, farmers light fires to clear the forest for farmland or grazing animals. Forests have become warmer and drier, so it is easier for fires to accidentally go out of control. In the USA, people are the cause of nearly 85 per cent of wildfires. Some people even deliberately start fires, which is a crime.

▶ *If someone carelessly throws a cigarette butt into dry grass, it can catch fire and quickly spread.*

ENVIRONMENTAL IMPACTS

Wildfires can destroy many trees – some tree species may be lost entirely. Fire-resistant species survive, but others die out, so there is less biodiversity (variety of species). Many creatures lose their habitat, or it is broken up by fire damage. This is a particular threat to animals already at risk or with limited habitats, such as koalas in Australia. Wildfire smoke contains toxic gases that can harm wildlife and humans, while the carbon dioxide given off during burning adds to global warming. Fires can damage the long-term health of the soil, so it is harder for the ecosystem to recover and for plants and animals to thrive there again.

◀ *A mother eastern grey kangaroo and her joey, survivors of a wildfire in Mallacoota, Australia.*

▶ *When firefighters cannot reach fires on land, they can fly over in aircraft to drop water or fire retardant – a mixture of chemicals that slows the spread of the fire.*

FIGHTING WILDFIRES

Fires are stopped by beating out the flames, dropping water from the air, and creating firebreaks.

FIREBREAKS

To stop wildfires from spreading, people sometimes deliberately burn a wide path through the land or forest to make a firebreak. With no trees or plants, a wildfire lacks fuel and may not be able to leap across the firebreak. Firebreaks can slow down the spread of a wildfire or stop it. Another way is to create green strips: areas planted with fire-resistant plants to reduce the spread of fire.

◀ *A firebreak can prevent a wildfire from spreading from one side of it to the other.*

FIRENADO!

When updraughts from the intense heat of a wildfire mix with violent winds, it can sometimes whip up a fire whirl – also called a fire devil or a firenado. These rotating columns of flame suck up smoke, gas and debris as they blaze paths of destruction. Fire whirls move unpredictably and make wildfires spread even faster. This firenado in the California hills was part of the Woolsey Fire of November 2018 that burned more than 39,000 hectares of land and caused over $6 billion of damage.

WARMING SEAS

Currents are movements of cold and warm water around the oceans. The oceans are becoming warmer, which is disrupting ecosystems.

▲ *Adélie penguins on an ice floe, a large area of melting ice, during the Antarctic summer.*

Ocean currents are warm or cold. The world's major currents move warm water around at the surface and cold water deep down in the oceans. In the tropical regions, the Sun heats the water. As the water flows towards the poles, it cools down. Cold, salty water sinks in the North Atlantic Ocean and in some areas off the coast of Antarctica. This cold water travels in deep currents around the world and rises to the surface again. Then the cycle repeats. The movement of heat through currents affects the climate.

THE IMPACT OF WARMING SEAS

Ice on land from ice sheets and glaciers melts and enters the ocean, making the sea level rise (see page 52). When sea ice melts, it does not make the sea level rise, but it adds fresh water to the ocean, making it less salty. The temperature and saltiness of the water drive the currents, so when either change, it can disrupt the currents. The climate in Western Europe is mild because the Atlantic Meridional Overturning Circulation (AMOC), currents in the Atlantic Ocean, bring warm water from tropical regions northwards. Fresh water from the melting ice sheets in Greenland is likely to weaken and slow down these currents, which could cool the climate of Western Europe.

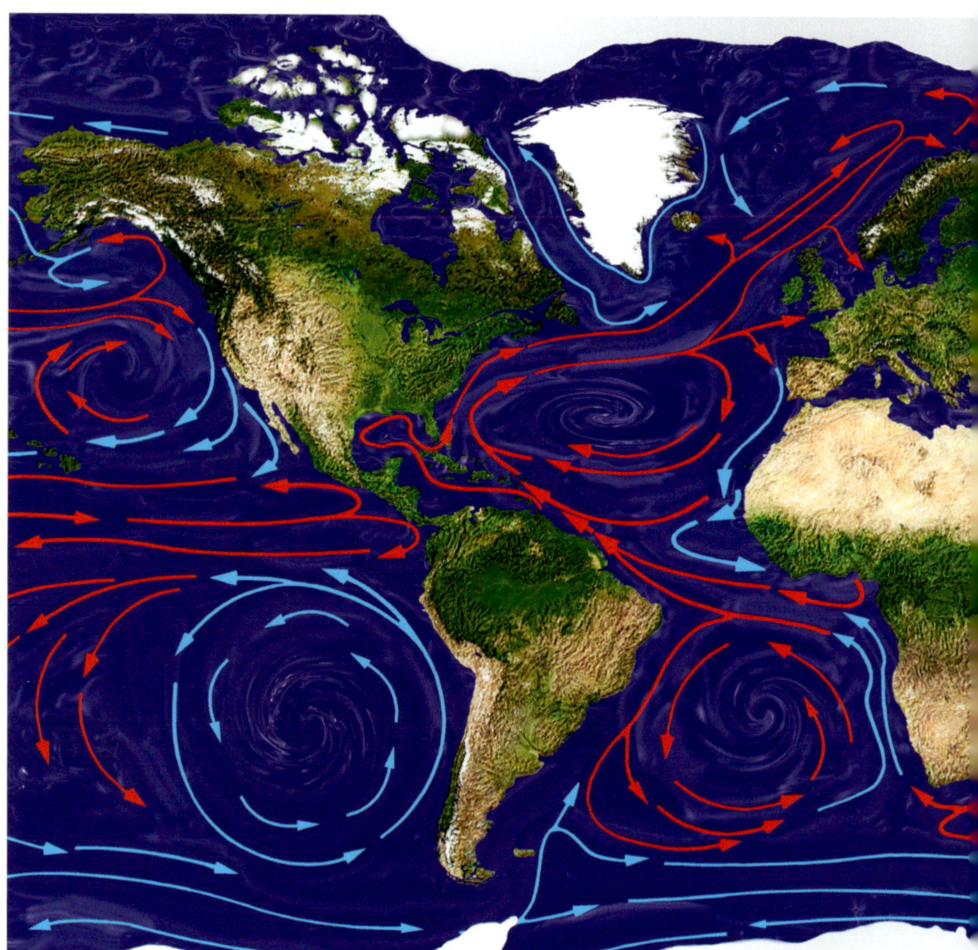

ICEBERG CALVING

Glaciers are ice masses that form near the North and South Poles. They move slowly towards the ocean, where icebergs (chunks of ice) break off. This is called calving. The icebergs may float on the currents for thousands of kilometres. When they reach warm waters, they melt.

▲ *A crack in an Antarctic glacier has cut across the ice shelf to the other side.*

▲ *Now the iceberg has separated from the coast and started to move away.*

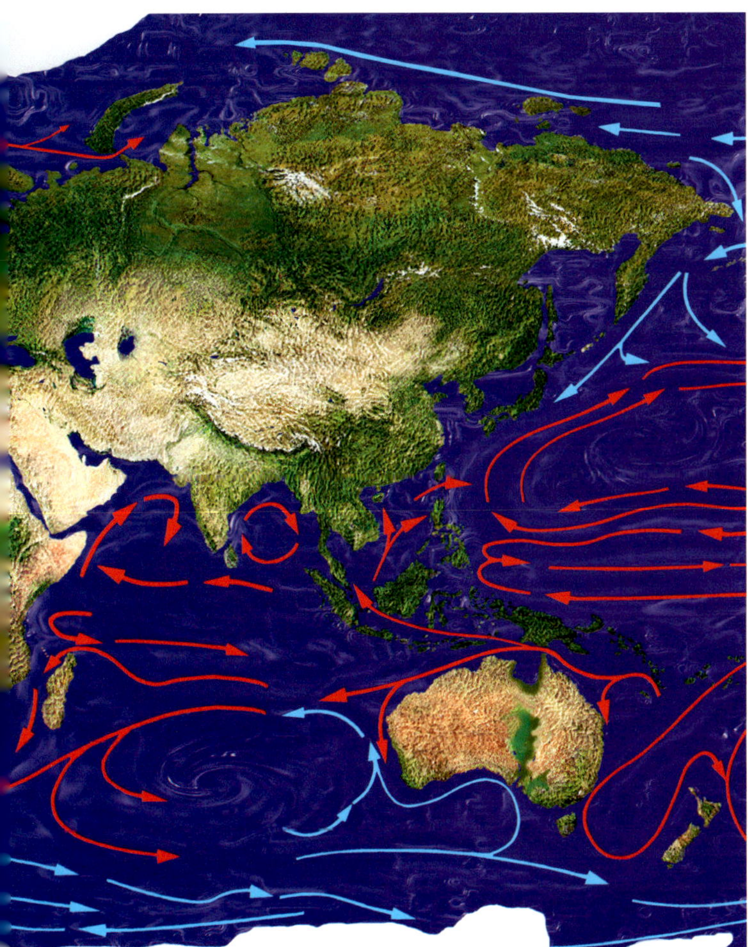

◀ *Cold currents (blue) tend to cause a dry climate on nearby land. Warm currents (red) usually bring warm weather and rain.*

EL NIÑO AND LA NIÑA

El Niño and La Niña are seasonal climate patterns in the Pacific Ocean that affect the world's weather for years. When the surface water in the eastern tropical Pacific Ocean becomes warmer than usual, El Niño occurs. The mass of warm water causes storms and increased rainfall in parts of the Americas but can lead to drought in Southeast Asia. When this part of the ocean becomes cooler than normal, La Niña happens. It usually causes more rain in Southeast Asia and drier weather in parts of the Americas.

▲ *During El Niño (left), California, USA, has storms; during La Niña, it suffers drought, making its lakes shrink (right).*

EL NIÑO WINTER IN NORTH AMERICA

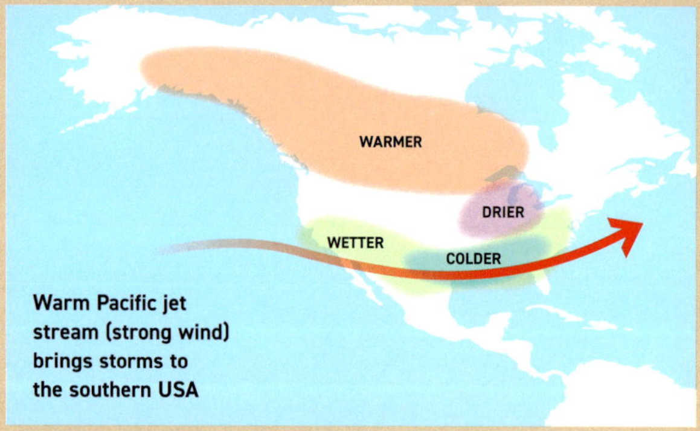

LA NIÑA WINTER IN NORTH AMERICA

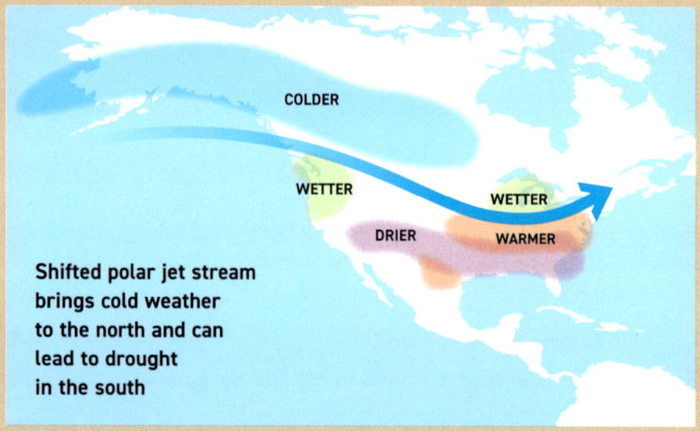

▲ *Coral in the Red Sea off Egypt was bleached in the summer of 2024 by high ocean temperatures.*

CORAL BLEACHING

Corals may look like plants, but they are animals, related to jellyfish. They often live in colonies (groups), and colonies joined together form coral reefs. Coral is found in many countries, but mostly in tropical seas. Many kinds have a special relationship with tiny plantlike algae. The algae live in the coral and produce around 90 per cent of the food that the coral need. When the sea temperature rises (or falls), it stresses the coral, which expels the algae, and so goes white. This process is called coral bleaching. Lacking food, the coral is greatly weakened and may die.

▲ *High tide in Tuvalu. This Pacific island is likely to be completely flooded by 2050.*

THE IMPACT OF RISING SEA LEVELS

Rising sea levels threaten life at coasts. Storm surges grow more intense, flooding is more common and tides are higher. Coastal ecosystems such as mangrove forests can be harmed. The floods dump salt on the land and make the groundwater salty, which can make it hard to grow crops. Coasts are home to large populations that may lose their homes and be forced to move inland. Many Asian countries such as Indonesia, Bangladesh and the Philippines are at risk. In Fiji, in the Pacific, buildings and farmland have already been destroyed by the ocean, and people have had to leave their villages.

MUCILAGE

Since the 1990s, mucilage has appeared in the Mediterranean region, including the Ligurian Sea in Italy and the Marmara Sea in Turkey. This slimy substance, known as 'sea snot', is thick and sticky. It forms because sea temperatures have become warmer and the water has too many nutrients, which allows tiny plantlike organisms called phytoplankton to grow rapidly. Pollution from homes and factories makes the problem worse. Mucilage smells bad and harms sea life. It covers the sea from the surface to 30 m (100 ft) deep, depriving sea creatures of oxygen. It kills animals such as oysters and mussels that cannot move, and harms fish larvae and eggs.

▶ *Red coral in the Mediterranean Sea in Italy covered with mucilage, which develops because of warmer seas and pollution.*

JET STREAMS

High in the atmosphere, 8–15 km (5–9 miles) above Earth, fast-moving currents of air called jet streams travel around the planet.

These currents occur when cold and warm air meet at the boundaries between major climate zones. The two main kinds are the strong polar jet streams near the North and South Poles, and two weaker ones around 30° latitude – the subtropical jet streams. Jet streams move air masses around, changing weather. For example, when the northern jet stream dips southwards, it brings freezing weather to temperate regions.

CHANGING JET STREAMS

The air currents' speed changes with the temperature. They are slow in summer and faster in winter, when the differences in air temperature are greater. Because Earth is growing warmer, the air currents are being disrupted. The polar regions are warming at a faster rate than other regions. This means the contrast in temperature that drives the jet streams has reduced, so they have become slower and less stable. For example, the polar jet stream is less cold, and ice has melted in Greenland. It has also become wavier and more unstable – it dips down deeper and rises higher – probably because of Arctic warming. When it swings up or down, it stays in the same place for longer, causing extreme weather, such as recent typhoons in East Asia.

▲ *Aircraft fly faster when travelling in the same direction as the fast-moving jet stream than when flying against it.*

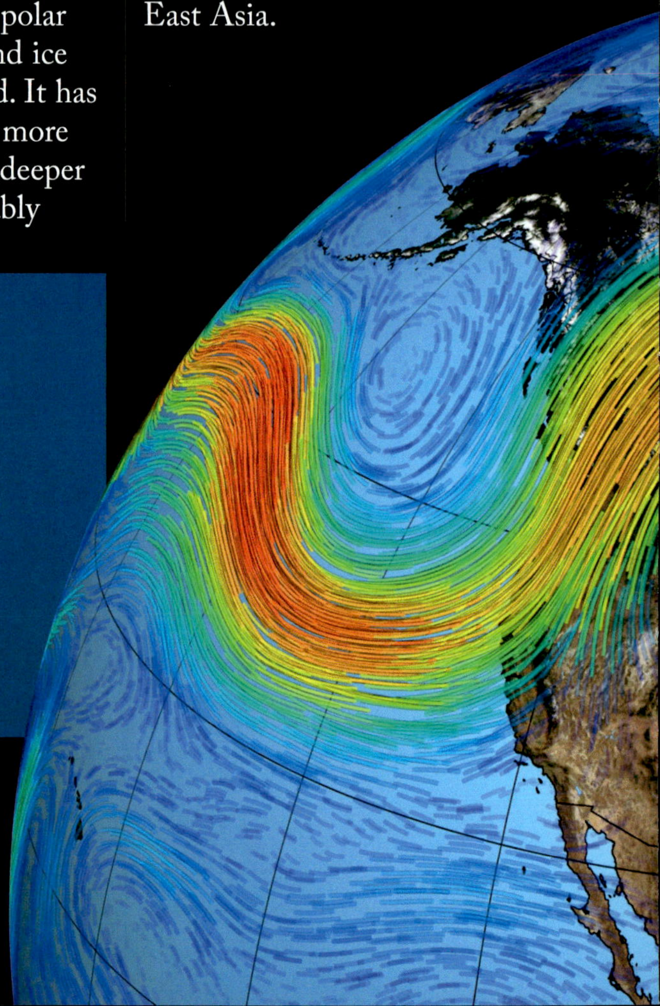

▲ *Tourists shelter from sudden heavy rain during a typhoon in Hangzhou, China, in July 2025.*

STABLE AND UNSTABLE JET STREAMS

The polar vortex is an area of low pressure and cold air around the poles, which weakens in summer and strengthens in winter. When it is strong and stable, the coldest polar air stays in the Arctic. When it weakens, warm air rises to the Arctic, and polar air sinks down.

▼ *The Arctic polar vortex is stable, so cold polar air stays in the Arctic.*

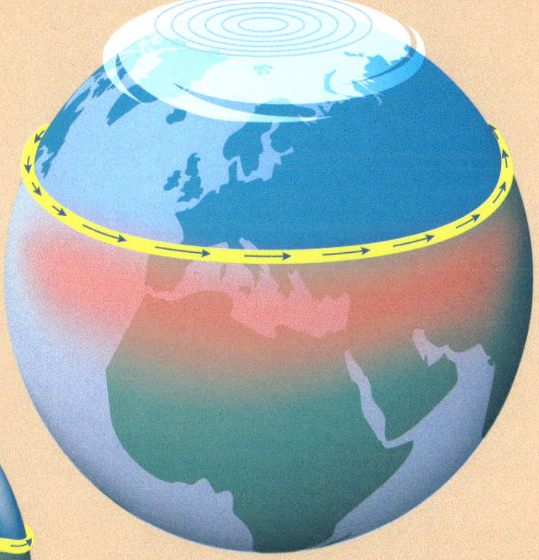

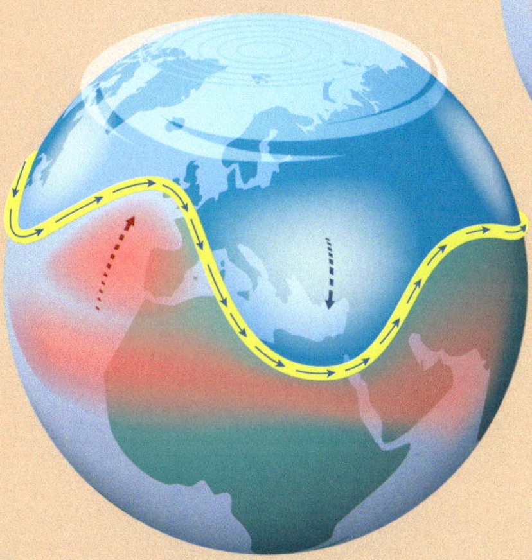

◀ *The Arctic polar vortex is wavy. Cold air moves south and lowers the temperature.*

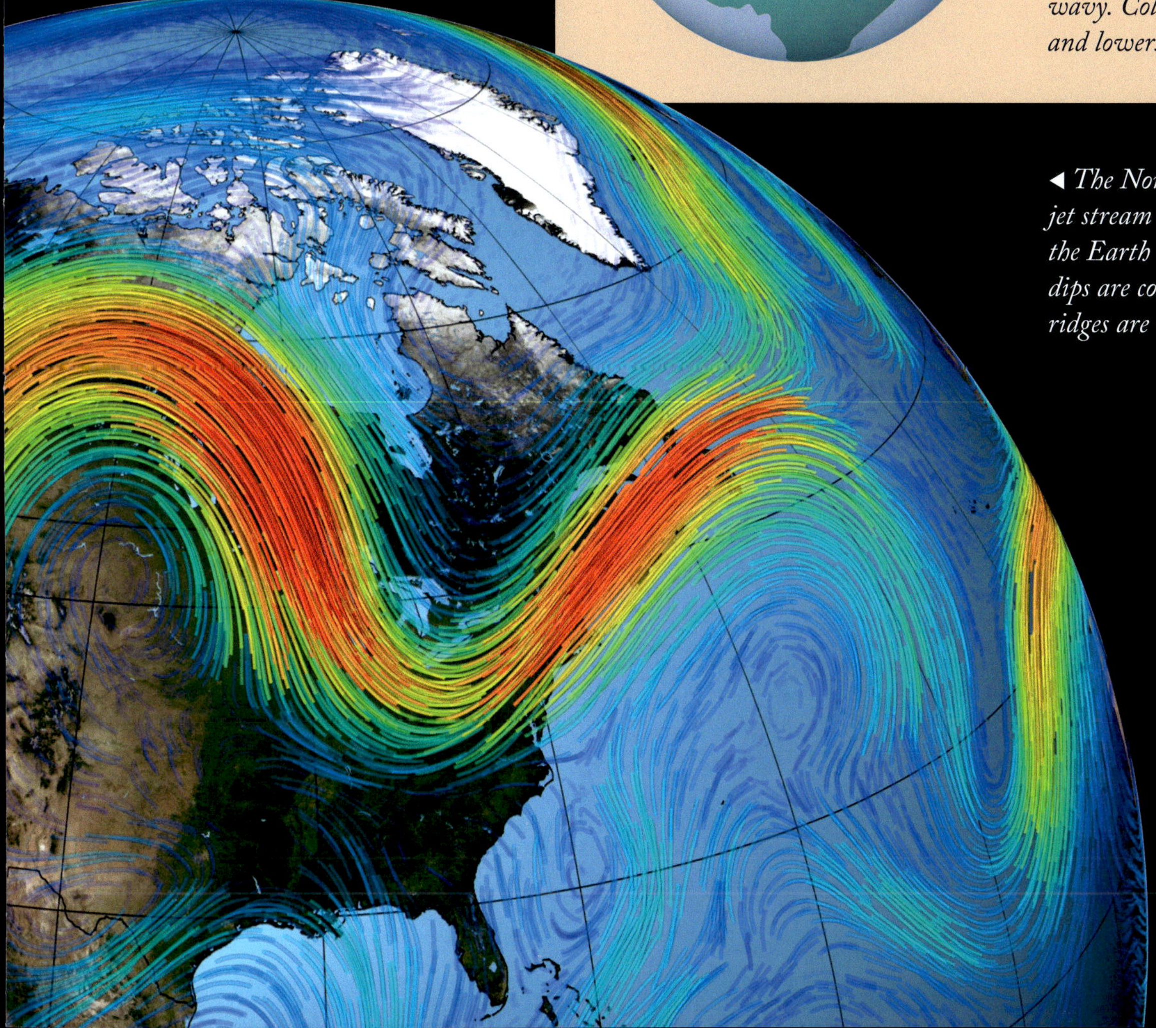

◀ *The Northern Hemisphere's polar jet stream moves eastwards because the Earth is always rotating. The dips are cold air sinking south; the ridges are warm air pushed north.*

EXTREME HEAT EVENTS

When a place has summer weather much hotter than normal for the time of year, an extreme heat event occurs.

Some regions naturally experience extreme heat. Areas around the Equator regularly reach scorching temps, and flat, low areas tend to be hotter than high mountain regions because the air is denser and Earth's surface radiates heat. Many extreme heat events are becoming more intense due to climate change. People with low incomes, especially in developing countries, are the most affected by these increasingly frequent extremes.

Hottest temperature recorded
Furnace Creek, Death Valley, USA, 1913

The highest recorded temperature ever was 56.7 °C (134 °F) on 10 July 1913 at California's Furnace Creek, so named for its boiling summer temperatures. Death Valley also holds the world record for the hottest month. For all of July 2018, the average daily temperature was 42.3 °C (108.1 °F). Death Valley reaches 86 m (282 ft) below sea level – one of the reasons it is so hot.

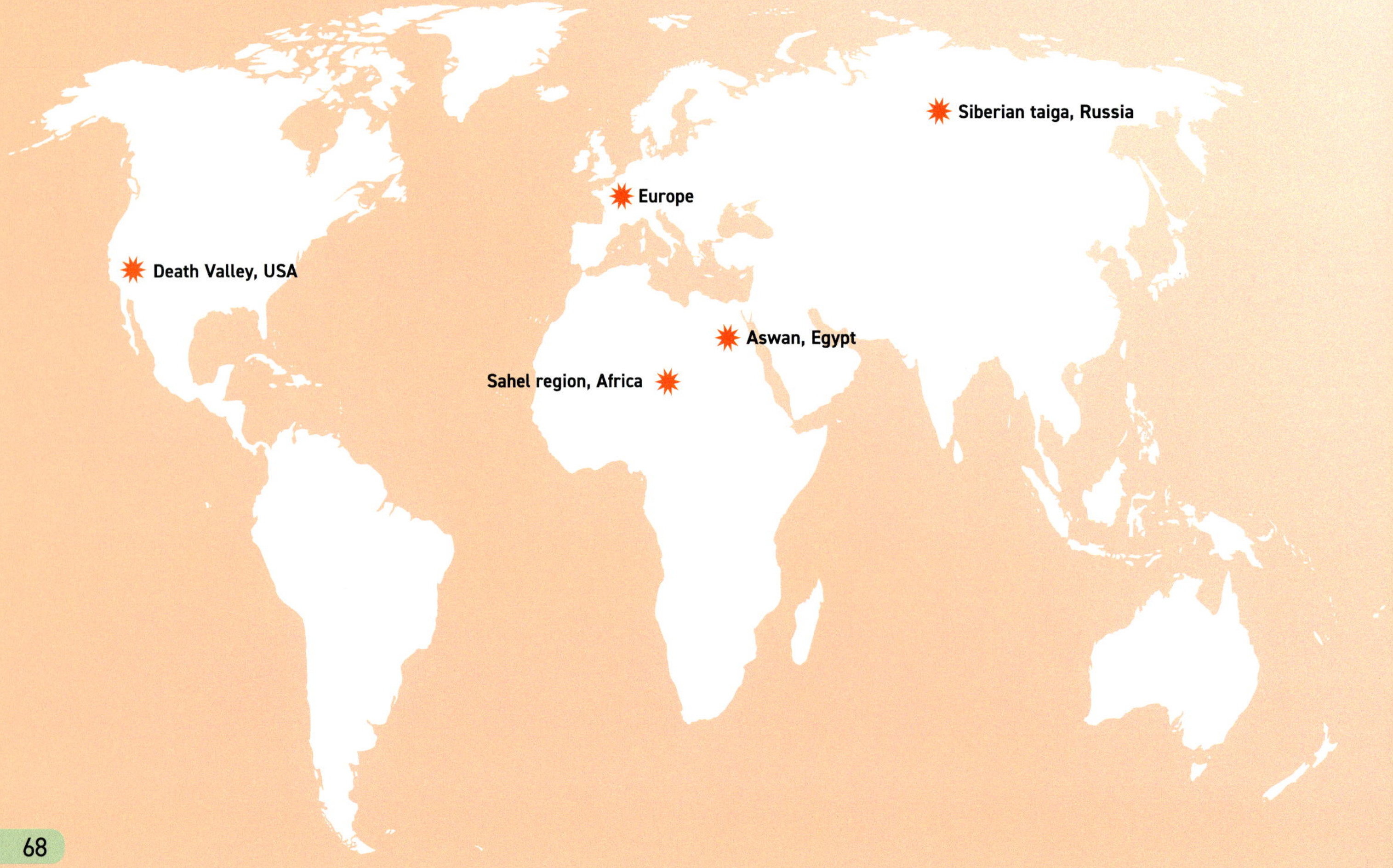

Driest hot places
Aswan, Egypt

Aswan in the Sahara Desert receives about 1 mm (0.04 in) of rain each year. It is hot all year round in the daytime. In August, the warmest month, the average temperature is 34.9 °C (94.8 °F). A few shrubs, grasses and night-feeding creatures like the fennec fox live there.

Most severe drought
Sahel region, Africa, 2012

South of the Sahara Desert, the Sahel stretches across Africa. A decades-long drought started in the 1960s. It is growing hotter, and the higher temperatures have made droughts worse. In the 2012 drought, farmers' crops died, and many had to sell livestock to buy food. Around 15 million people went hungry.

Worst wildfires
Siberian taiga, Russia, 2003

In 2003, during an extremely hot summer in Europe, wildfires started by lightning burned 22 million hectares (55 million acres) of trees in the northern forests of Siberia. Since then, Arctic warming has caused decreased rainfall, drying soils and drought, increasing the risk of wildfires.

Extreme heatwaves
Europe, 2020s

Since 2020, Europe has suffered severe heatwaves, causing thousands of heat-related deaths. These events are linked to Arctic warming and heat domes: when high pressure stays over an area for days or weeks, trapping hot air. In July 2024, Athens, Greece, had minimum temperatures of over 30 °C (86 °F) for 12 days. In June 2025, temperatures reached 46 °C (115 °F) in Spain and Portugal. France had dramatic temperature rises, too.

3 EXTREME COLD

NORMAL WINTER COLD

Waking up to find a blanket of snow outside with the promise of snowball fights and tobogganing can be exciting, but this seasonal spectacle is becoming rarer.

▲ *Most snowflakes have six sides and six points, but no two snowflakes are the same.*

Around the world, winter can have different meanings. Many parts of Africa experience dry days or mild, wet ones during winter, which is from June to August there. Temperate countries, such as those in Europe, that sit between the polar circles and the tropics have short days with average temperatures near freezing. If temperatures drop lower, snow may fall, which happens more frequently closer to the poles.

WINTER WARMER

Snowfall does not need to be heavy to disrupt daily life. Schools and colleges sometimes close. Homes and workplaces may require extra heating in cold weather, increasing gas and electricity usage. Snowploughs may be needed to clear snow or lorries may scatter a salt-based grit to prevent icy roads.

Snow does have benefits, though. As well as being fun to play in, it provides an insulating layer that protects plants and animals underground from deep frost and harsh winds. Melting snow helps break up soil and keeps the ground moist in areas that are in danger of wildfires.

Climate change will result in less snow falling in most areas. Data from 244 US cities shows winters have warmed by an average of 2.2°C (3.9°F) since 1970, a trend seen worldwide, with the number of cold days and nights falling. Precipitation will fall more as rain, not snow, if temperatures continue to rise. Cold snaps will still occur, but they'll be much less frequent.

FROST DAMAGE

A field twinkling with frost may be a beautiful sight, but it is not one welcomed by farmers. Frost can damage crops because it causes water in the plants to freeze, expand and rupture their cell walls. Many farmers spray their crops to stop frost forming.

▶ *Some hardy plants, including brambles, can survive in temperatures as low as -18°C (0°F).*

WET WEATHER

Precipitation is the word given to water that falls from the sky. It can take different forms – in many places, rain and a light rain called drizzle are the forms most often seen. It can also be solid – such as snow. In winter, most precipitation in places with temperate climates starts as snow because it is so cold higher in the atmosphere. If the temperature is warmer closer to the ground, the snow can melt.

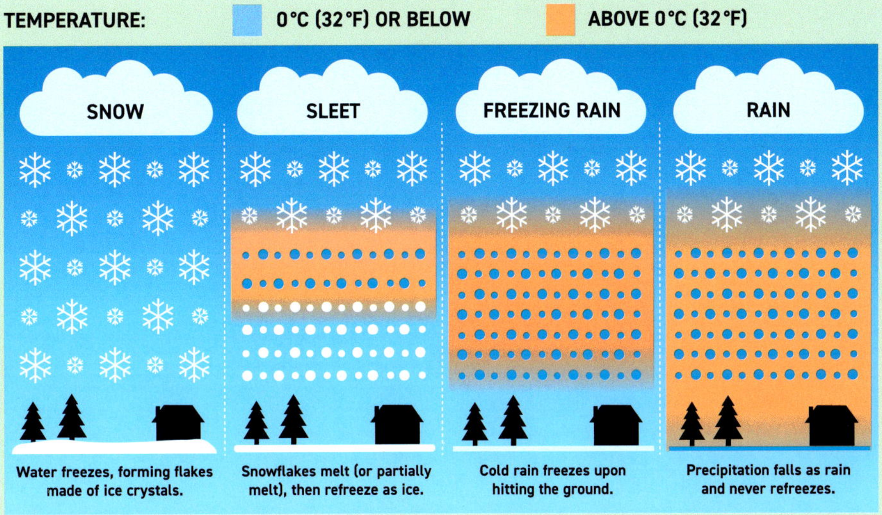

▲ *This illustration shows how snowfall is affected by warmer temperatures. When snow melts, it can refreeze, but if the ground is warm enough, it will land as rain.*

▼ *Sudden snowfall may be hazardous, but a thin dusting can create an appealing winter wonderland that improves mental health, forging a connection with nature.*

COLD WAVES

A sudden plunge in air temperature in a short space of time, cold waves can bring unexpected harsh, wintry conditions that last for days.

The opposite of a heatwave, a cold wave sees people crank up the heating instead of the air conditioning. Also called a cold snap, it often begins with an extreme winter event, such as an ice storm or a blizzard. Because it happens so quickly, there is little time to get prepared for the wintry storms. Homes may lose heat and power, and dangerous driving conditions, can result from cold waves.

ARCTIC AIR

A cold wave in most places means a rapid drop in temperature within 24 hours that lasts for at least two days. Some countries have other criteria. In the UK, for instance, the average temperature must fall below 2°C (36°F) for 48 hours and there must be snow and ice over a large area.

In the northern half of the planet, cold air comes from the Arctic regions of northern Canada and Asia. In Earth's southern half, cold waves start in Antarctica and the Southern Ocean. In North America, chilly Arctic air is carried by changes in the jet stream, a thin zone of strong winds that can travel around 177 km/h (110 mph). Cold waves in Europe are also brought by disturbances in the jet stream, redirecting air from Siberia or other parts of the Arctic.

▼ *Snow blowers clear blocked roads by pulling in snow with a paddle called an auger and directing it several metres away using a high-speed fan.*

SEVERE SNAPS

Cold waves are more than just a hindrance; they can be a major hazard to health, transport networks and farming. In 2018, parts of the UK were brought to a standstill by a cold snap nicknamed 'The Beast from the East'. Night-time temperatures fell to -8°C (17.6°F) and heavy snow cut off villages. Some areas saw 50 cm (19.7 in) of snow, made worse by strong winds causing snow drifts. Central and eastern Asia suffered from a record cold snap in 2023. The northernmost city in China, Mohe, had a low temperature of -53°C (-63.4°F) in January. The average temperature there for that time of year is -15°C (5°F).

◀ *Cold snaps almost always take temperatures below the freezing point of water, or 0°C (32°F). This outdoor thermometer couldn't even measure the coldest recorded temperatures, which can reach lower than -60°C (-90°F).*

COLD FRONTS

A boundary between two masses of air is called a weather front. The greater the difference between the temperatures of the two masses, the more powerful the front. A cold front occurs when a mass of cold air moves in, pushing under a mass of warm air. This often brings lots of precipitation.

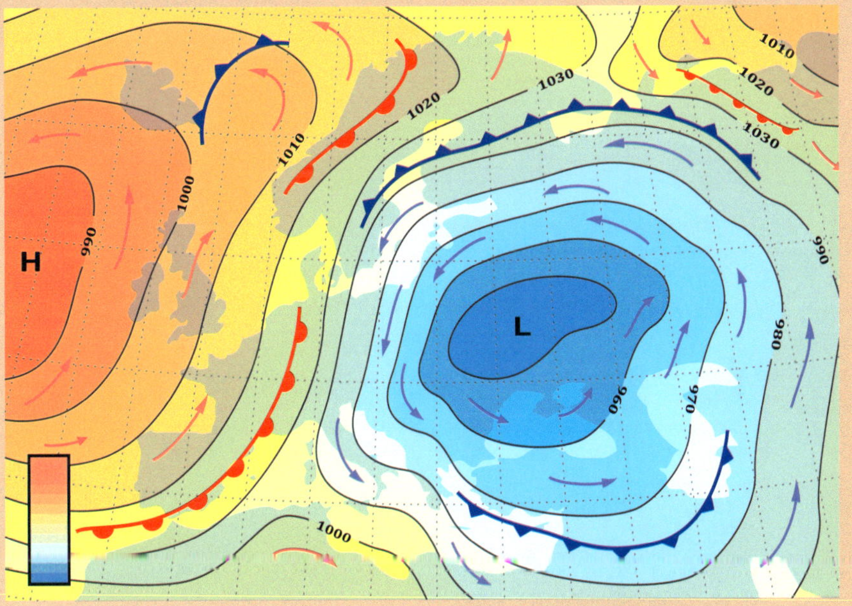

▶ *On a weather map, a cold front is shown as a blue line with blue triangles, which point in the direction that the front is moving.*

WHAT IS SNOW?

When it gets very cold, water vapour in clouds freezes into tiny crystals of ice. More crystals grow around them to make snowflakes. Snowfall is made of single ice crystals and snowflakes. Snow is powdery if it falls through cold, dry air, but wet if the air is moist.

WHAT IS SLEET?

That depends on where you live. In parts of Europe, sleet is frozen precipitation that has begun to melt before it hits the ground, so it falls as a mix of snow and rain. In the US, sleet refers to snowflakes that melt into rain, then freeze into tiny pellets of ice that bounce off the ground.

WHAT IS FROST?

When water vapour, a gas, lands on an object that is at 0°C (32°F) or lower, it changes into a liquid. The water droplets then freeze into tiny, white ice crystals that we call frost. It often forms during the night, when temperatures are lower, and melts during the day.

▲ *Snow chains fit over car tyres for driving in winter. If a road is covered by snow or ice, the chains provide extra grip by biting into the surface.*

EXTREME COLD EQUIPMENT

A heavy snowfall can leave people stranded in their homes or their vehicles, so it pays to be prepared. Keeping items like an ice scraper, shovel, warm blanket and first aid kit in your car could save lives. A mobile phone can be used to call for help, while apps such as a torch and maps are useful, too. A portable power bank to keep the phone charged is also important. Water and food are vital, and a supply of bottled water and tinned or freeze-dried goods can be stored for a long time.

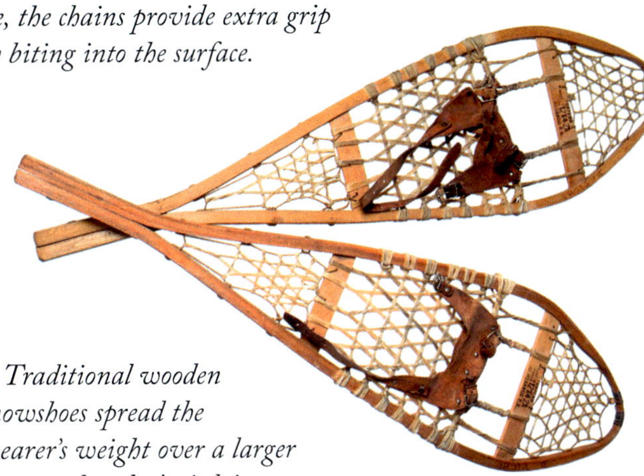

▶ *Traditional wooden snowshoes spread the wearer's weight over a larger area, so they don't sink in snow.*

▼ *Building up clothes in layers is wise, starting from long underwear and ending with outerwear that protects from precipitation to keep the other layers dry.*

COLD-WEATHER CLOTHES

Clothing is key to surviving extreme cold and preventing conditions such as frostbite. Fabrics that allow sweat to escape but also trap air warmed by the body are best. Cotton, which holds moisture, is not ideal. Hands and feet feel cold because more warm blood is pumped to vital organs instead, so they should always be kept covered.

ICE STORMS

Even a gentle snowfall can turn deadly if it freezes at ground level, resulting in a build-up of ice that disrupts power supplies and cuts off communities.

Driving on an icy road can be terrifying when the wheels skid and the vehicle slides out of control. That's just one of many hazards created by an ice storm. If your car is left outside, it could become totally enclosed in ice. A build-up of ice can also increase the weight of tree branches by 30 times, causing them to break. It can even split trunks in half!

CHANGING STATES

An ice storm might sound like chunks of ice falling from the sky, but the reality is a bit different. This slippery hazard occurs when a warm layer of air sits above a colder layer. Ice or snow passes through the warmer layer and melts into liquid. The droplets then meet the colder air, becoming freezing rain, but still staying liquid. When it strikes the ground or an object that is below 0°C (32°F), it freezes on contact.

If 0.65 cm (0.25 in) of ice builds up, this is usually called an ice storm. If there is 1.3 cm (0.5 in) of ice or more, damage to property and powerlines can be expected, especially if there is strong wind. Thick ice can remain a hazard for several weeks, especially if sub-zero temperatures continue, because it will melt very slowly.

◄ *This lighthouse at the St. Joseph North Pier in Michigan, USA, still manages to shine its warning beacon following an ice storm.*

▲ *If a power pylon is brought down in an ice storm, it can increase the risk of fires and electrocution, as well as blocking transport networks.*

because it will melt very slowly. If it melts but the temperature falls again, this can lead to another danger on roads called black ice. Black ice is difficult to see because it is clear instead of white, and it prevents tyres from gripping the road.

POWER PROBLEMS

Ice storms can be devastating. In 1940, London, England, experienced its second coldest January of the 20th century. The River Thames froze over and ice up to 30 cm (12 in) thick brought down branches and power lines. With Britain already facing the early effects of World War II, it was a challenging time for millions of people. Another ice storm passed across southeast Canada and northeast USA in January 1998. The ice measured 10 cm (4 in) thick and caused around $4 billion (£740 million) worth of damage. Hundreds of thousands of people had no electricity – some even waited weeks before it was restored.

ICICLE DANGER

Icicles are spikes that form when water drips from an object in sub-zero temperatures and freezes. They can often be seen hanging from the edges of buildings. If the temperature begins to rise, icicles start to thaw and crash down. Anyone unlucky enough to be standing underneath may be injured if the ice hits them. A large icicle can even break bones.

▶ *Heavy icicles, such as the ones on this house in Wisconsin, USA, can damage walls, collapse roofs, and even injure or kill people.*

EPIC ICE

The world's biggest freshwater lake by volume, Siberia's Lake Baikal is covered with ice for about five months a year. The ice, which can be up to 1.5 m (5 ft) thick, is famous for its turquoise and green colours, and for cracking into spectacular blocks and shards. Cars can drive over it in the winter, but unpredictable weather has led to many accidents, with people and vehicles plunging through the ice. The lake can also experience 'ice tsunamis', with strong winds casting massive sheets of ice onto shore.

BLIZZARDS

When heavy snow is blown by strong winds, it results in a blizzard. It's easy to get lost in these winter storms that last for hours.

With snow swirling around, it is very difficult to see where you're going, which is why car accidents are common in blizzards. When visibility is so bad that it's impossible to identify nearby objects, or even see where the ground and sky meet, it is known as a whiteout. Sometimes this type of dangerous storm can happen when no flakes are falling. In a ground blizzard, strong winds whip up already fallen snow.

▲ *Drivers risk being stranded in a blizzard. Taking a hat, gloves, warm clothing, a high-vis jacket, sleeping bag, shovel and tow rope is recommended in case roads become impassable.*

WINTER WINDS

In many places around the world, a blizzard requires winds of 56 km/h (35 mph) or more, with visibility reduced to less than 400 m (a quarter of a mile) for at least three hours. In the UK, blizzard conditions indicate winds of 48 km/h (30 mph) or greater, and visibility of 200 m (660 ft) or less. However, in the extremes of Antarctica, blizzards refer to winds that blow over the edge of the ice plateau and travel at around 160 km/h (100 mph). That's faster than any land animal can run!

Blizzards develop when there is a difference in air pressure between two places. Cold air exerts higher pressure than warm air, so when they meet, the warm air rises over the cold air and forms wind. The more quickly the warm air rises, the stronger the wind becomes.

▶ *Anyone that has to go outside in a blizzard must be dressed for the weather, wearing layers of clothes that expel sweat underneath a waterproof coat and trousers.*

▼ *A blizzard can trap hundreds of people in different locations, resulting in a race against time for emergency service teams to rescue them in dangerous conditions.*

STRONGER STORMS

Extreme snowstorms can have disastrous effects, especially in places where they aren't expected. In 1972, a week-long blizzard in Iran left hundreds of villages buried under up to 8 m (26 ft) of snow, killing 4,000 people. In 1993, the so-called 'Storm of the Century' wrecked havoc across 26 US states. Southern states like Tennessee saw a record 1.5 m (5 ft) of snow.

Scientists have predicted that climate change will lead to more intense blizzards, even though winters are getting shorter. The atmosphere is becoming warmer, which means the air contains more moisture that will fall as snow in sub zero temperatures. Warmer temperatures can also be responsible for stronger winds. Compared to the 1950s, there are now almost four times as many blizzards in the US.

STORM ELLIOTT

A major winter storm caused havoc in most of the US and parts of Canada for five days in December 2022. Blizzards were reported in several states during Storm Elliott. More than 5,700 flights in or out of the US before Christmas had to be cancelled. Snyder in New York saw 99 cm (39 in) of snowfall, while a 243 km/h (151 mph) gust of wind was reported in New Hampshire.

▲ *This storm forecast map for 23 December 2022 shows areas with air temperatures ranging from 10°C (50°F) above average (orange) to -25°C (-13°F) below average (dark blue).*

EXTREME HAIL

Large chunks of solid ice travelling at high speeds can cause immense damage on impact, crashing through roofs and uprooting crops in fields.

A familiar sight worldwide, hail occurs in every continent except Antarctica. It is more intense in some areas. Places far away from seas and oceans, such as central USA, and mountain regions, such as the southern Alps in Europe, see hail more often. Stones can vary widely in size, but a threat is issued when there is a greater than 26 per cent chance of golf ball-sized hail or a more than 16 per cent chance of baseball-sized stones.

HOW HAIL FORMS

Hailstones are created inside thunderstorms. They are formed from supercooled water – or water below its normal freezing point of 0°C (32°F) that is still liquid. It is carried upwards by warm updrafts, where the air is even colder. When the supercooled water comes into contact with something, such as a dust particle, it freezes around it. Gravity causes the ice to fall inside the cloud before an updraft lifts it again. More supercooled water freezes around the stone, and the cycle begins again. New layers are added, creating a structure similar to the rings inside a tree trunk. Large stones may contain clear and cloudy layers, based on how quickly the ice froze.

◀ *Hailstones are usually round or cone-shaped, although larger ones can be covered with icy spikes.*

▲ *This supercell thunderstorm in South Dakota, USA, produced the largest confirmed hailstone in 2010. It had a diameter of 20 cm (7.9 in), similar to the width of a dinner plate.*

HEAVY HAIL

Finally, the hailstones become so heavy they cannot be lifted by the updraft, and they fall to the ground. Larger hail tends to fall quicker. A stone 2.5 cm (1 in) across travels at up to 40 km/h (25 mph). A cricket-ball sized stone, 7.2 cm (2.8 in) wide, could fall twice as quickly – or even faster. Hail this size in Arizona, USA, caused $2.8 billion (£1.8 billion) of damage in 2010. Bigger hailstones have been recorded – the heaviest known fell during a 1986 storm in Bangladesh. It weighed 1 kg (2.2 lb), about the same as a pineapple. History's deadliest hailstorm occurred in 1888, killing several hundred people and 1,600 livestock in India.

THUNDERSTORM + THERMALS = HAIL

Hail is formed inside tall cumulonimbus clouds, which are associated with severe weather, such as heavy rain and lightning. Summer thermals are also needed – these rising currents of air are created by warm weather. The diagram below shows the updraft that lifts hailstones to the top of the cloud, where they become too heavy to be supported and fall. Supercell thunderstorms have a rotating updraft, resulting in bigger hailstones.

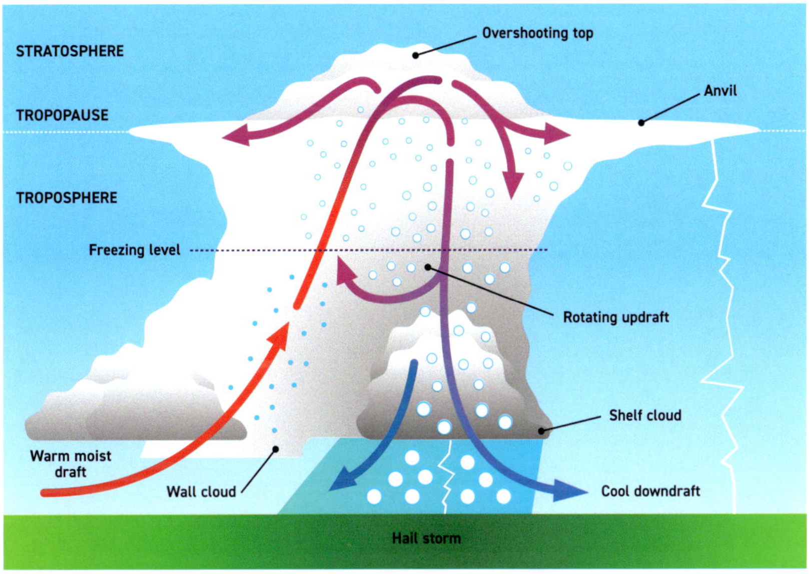

▲ *The updraft carrying the hail rises until it meets a layer called the tropopause, forcing the cloud to spread out, creating its classic anvil shape at the top.*

▲ *Hailstones can smash car windscreens. If a storm starts, drivers are advised to pull over or drive to a nearby covered area, such as a garage forecourt.*

AVALANCHES

A fast-moving mass of snow and ice, an avalanche can travel quicker than a car on the motorway, uprooting trees and crushing villages in its path.

Some people think that loud noises cause avalanches, but that happens very rarely. It's usually extra weight, such as a heavy snowfall, that starts one. The key factors are the amount of snow and ice on the ground (which is called the snowpack), the landscape and the weather. A trigger is also needed – in 90 per cent of avalanches involving people, it is humans that are the trigger. Hundreds of people are trapped by avalanches every year.

WEATHER WARNINGS

Avalanches can travel at speeds of up to 161 km/h (100 mph), fast enough to move over flat ground for short distances. They can start on any slope with an incline of 30° or more, and at any time, although most occur in winter. Scientists try to predict when avalanches will happen by studying layers in

▼ *In July 2024, an avalanche at Khan Tengri mountain in Central Asia was followed by a second, deadlier one, just three hours later.*

snow caused by different events such as rain and freezing and examining how the layers interact. However, weather conditions can rapidly change, so avalanche forecasters warn people to always be prepared. Travelling earlier in the day is best because, as snow melts in the sun, it makes wet, loose avalanches more likely. If you're in an avalanche's path, experts recommend climbing a tree or moving in a swimming motion. Once an avalanche stops, the snow hardens like concrete.

TYPES OF AVALANCHE

There are various types of avalanches, which are named after their formation or their appearance. Some of these are shown below. A slab avalanche is a large, complete piece of snow and is the deadliest type. A loose snow avalanche begins at a single point and widens out as it travels downwards. A glide avalanche occurs when the entire snowpack slides down instead of one weak layer. An avalanche can even change type as it moves – a slab avalanche can break up and mix with air to become powder snow.

EXPLOSIVE SITUATIONS

In areas where lives may be at risk from avalanches, they can be started artificially. Explosives, such as dynamite, are thrown by hand or fired from blast cannons to control the movement of snow safely. This is useful in areas that are difficult to reach, such as steep slopes and rock faces. It also helps keep roads clear after heavy snowfall. Ski resorts might launch rounds of artillery to make sure their slopes are safe for winter sports before visitors arrive. Patrols in some ski areas discharge thousands of hand charges every year to control avalanches.

◀ *Bomb experts at the Val Thorens ski resort in France use dynamite for avalanche maintenance.*

SNOW STOPPERS

Barriers, also called snow bridges, can help stop an avalanche's progress. They are often built on slopes that lack natural obstacles, such as trees, and are common in the Alps mountain range. The barriers need to be secured deep into the rock to withstand the weight and strength of an avalanche. Flexible barriers made from steel wire mesh keep the snowpack in place at an avalanche's starting zone. Rigid barriers made from steel, wood or concrete are installed further down the slope to stop an avalanche's progress or divert it to a safe place, away from inhabited areas.

▼ *It is almost impossible to ski faster than most avalanches, so carrying essential equipment is vital.*

BAG FOR LIFE

The chances of surviving an avalanche are increased by carrying an airbag. When a toggle is pulled, it inflates and helps the victim stay close to the snow's surface. Carrying a transceiver is also important. This electronic device will send a radio signal to rescuers, allowing them to pinpoint where someone is buried. Experts also recommend spitting into the snow if trapped. The saliva will be pulled down by gravity, indicating that the surface is in the opposite direction.

▲ *A shovel for digging, electronic transceiver and foldable probe for testing the snowpack are standard kit for rescuers.*

AVALANCHE RESCUE

In the race to locate an avalanche victim, time is key. If they are rescued within 10 minutes, they have a higher than 90 per cent chance of survival. The quickest rescues are often carried out by travel companions who are already at the location. When search-and-rescue teams are alerted, they have experience, equipment – and avalanche dogs. These clever canines have spent up to three years training to work in different types of snow and to detect human scent.

EXTREME COLD EVENTS

Whether it means coping with huge snowfalls or freezing temperatures, humans manage to find a way to exist in some hostile environments.

Some areas are too brutally cold for people to live there. No one has a permanent home in Antarctica, but scientists and researchers do work there for months. Canada and Russia are two of the coldest countries, although Greenland, a territory of Denmark with a population of around 57,000, is colder than both of them with an average annual temperature of -18.5°C (-1.3°F). However, for real chills, take a trip to these places…

Coldest town
Verkhoyansk, Sakha, Russia

Known for its gold and tin mining, this northern Russian town's temperature once fell to -67.6°C (-89.7°F). Verkhoyansk holds the world record for the greatest annual temperature range. In January, the average is -49°C (-56.2°F), but in summer the thermometer can climb to more than 30°C (86°F).

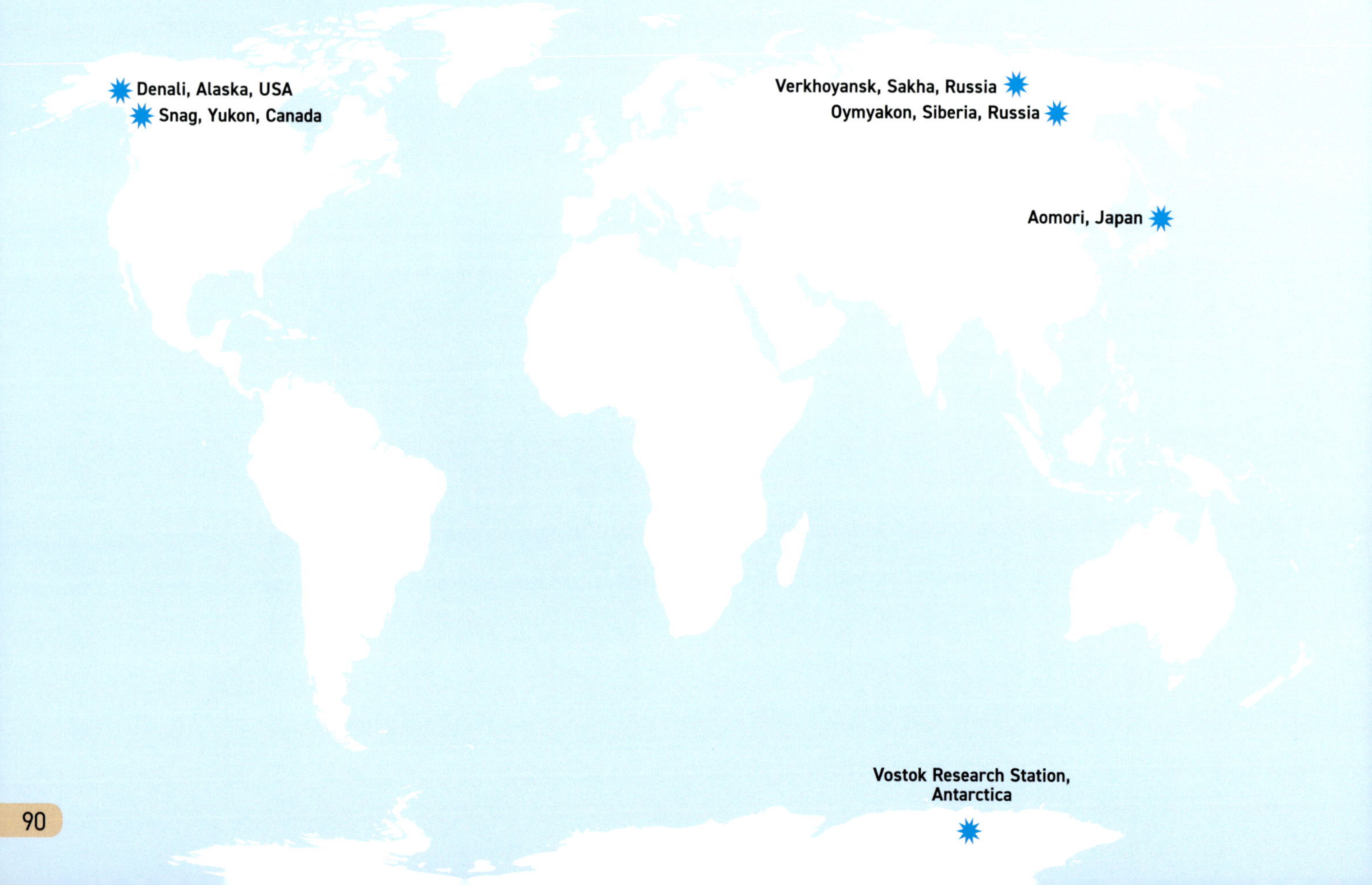

Coldest permanently inhabited place
Oymyakon, Siberia, Russia

Between December and February, temperatures in this village average -48°C (-54.4°F). In 1933, Oymyakon recorded a record low of -67.7°C (-89.9°F). Planes cannot land for part of the year, but the village school only closes when temperatures drop below -55°C (-67°F).

Coldest temperature in North America
Snag, Yukon, Canada

In 1947, the tiny village of Snag was used as an emergency landing strip for planes and as a weather station. When researchers saw the temperature was -62.8°C (-81°F), which was lower than their thermometer could measure, they sent the equipment away to be checked!

Coldest place
Vostok Research Station, Antarctica

The coldest temperature ever recorded at ground level was a glacial -89.2°C (-128.6°F). Oddly, the Vostok Research Station is also one of the sunniest places on the planet. In December, there can be more than 22 hours of sunlight in a day. Antarctica might experience even lower temperatures – satellites have recorded surface ice at -93.2°C (-135.8°F).

Snowiest city
Aomori, Japan

Between November and April, Japan's Aomori is usually covered by a blanket of snow that builds up in banks. This is when most of the city's annual snowfall of 792 cm (312 in) occurs. Strong winter winds pick up moisture from the Mutsu Bay coastline and drop it as snow on Aomori when they hit the Hakkōda Mountains.

Coldest mountain
Denali, Alaska, USA

North America's tallest mountain is also the world's coldest. Mount Denali rises 6,190 m (20,310 ft) above sea level, and its peak is covered with snow all year round. Temperatures around -73°C (-99.4°F) have been recorded, although the wind makes it feel like -83°C (-117.4°F). Only half the mountaineers who attempt to climb Denali reach the top.

4 DANGEROUS WINDS

HOW WIND WORKS

Without wind we would have no weather. Air moving around Earth spreads essential moisture, distributes seeds and provides renewable energy.

Solar radiation warms our planet, but some areas absorb more heat than others. The oceans warm up more slowly than the land, while the poles receive less sunlight. This affects the temperature of the air above, with less dense warm air rising, and more dense cool air moving downwards to take its place. This movement of air from areas of high pressure to low pressure is what we call wind.

▲ *Barometers record changes in atmospheric pressure and can help predict local weather changes. Low pressure indicates cold and rain, while high pressure indicates settled conditions.*

DEFLECTED CURRENTS

Warm air builds over the Equator and forms currents that rise but do not head directly to the cooler poles. The air currents are deflected due to Earth's rotation, by what is known as the Coriolis force. In the Northern Hemisphere, air currents are shifted to the right, making anticlockwise turns around areas of low pressure and clockwise turns around areas of high pressure. The currents are diverted in the opposite directions in the Southern Hemisphere. These air movements are Earth's prevailing or planetary winds. The force and direction of the winds can also be altered by coastlines, mountains, valleys and tall buildings, creating local wind and weather patterns.

▶ *Wind can be harnessed by turbines, which turn generators and provide a clean and renewable source of electrical energy.*

HIGHS AND LOWS

Cold air sinks due to its higher density, forming areas of high atmospheric pressure below with winds circulating outwards. These weather systems are called anticyclones and usually bring fine weather. Rising warm air results in low pressure below. The air cools as it reaches higher altitudes and water vapour condenses to form clouds. Areas of inward-circulating winds at low pressure are called cyclones.

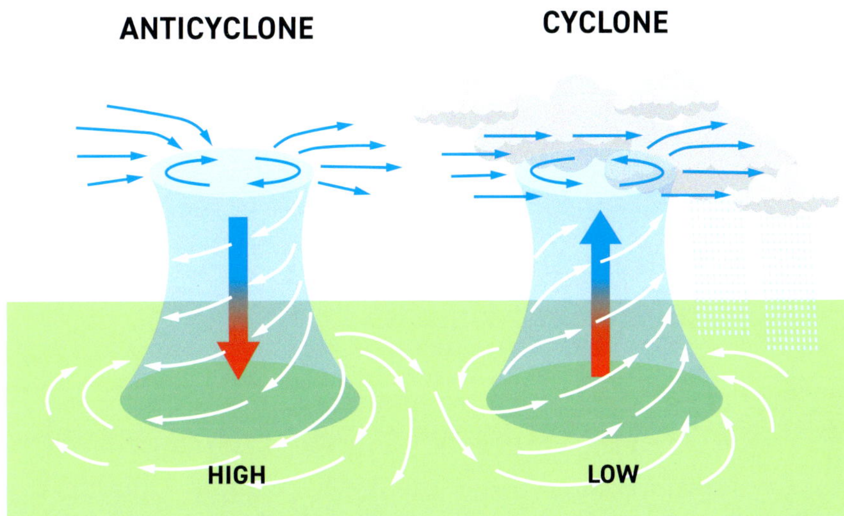

▲ *Differences in temperature between land and sea are responsible for coastal breezes blowing onto land during the daytime.*

FRONTS AND JET STREAMS

Regions of high and low air pressure are outlined on weather maps with isobars. The forward-moving edge of a large air mass is called a front. Weather forecasts may refer to a warm front approaching, as an area of high pressure moves in, replacing cooler air. Winds are defined by their origin – a north-westerly is a wind coming from the northwest.

Wind fronts may extend upwards for many kilometres. In the stratosphere, or upper atmosphere, winds called jet streams may blow at speeds up to 400 km/h (250 mph). Commercial aircraft pilots choose to fly here, where there is little turbulence. Flying in the direction of a jet stream, known as a tailwind, can speed up a flight and save pilots fuel. Flying against a headwind can cause delays.

THE BEAUFORT SCALE

Wind speed or strength is measured using the Beaufort scale, from the calmest conditions to the most violent storms.

The bigger the air-pressure difference, the faster the air moves and the greater the wind speed. The speed of the wind is measured by meteorologists using a spinning-cup device called an anemometer, while a wind vane records its direction. A wind's strength can be described using the Beaufort scale, based on a measurement system standardised by the British naval officer Sir Francis Beaufort in 1805.

ABOVE AND BEYOND

Originally designed to aid sailors, the Beaufort scale now records the effects of different strengths of wind over both land and sea. The scale is typically shown as ranging from 0 (for calm conditions) to 12 (for violent storms), but it officially goes up to 17, with the last five numbers used to measure tropical cyclones. The fastest storm wind on record was produced by Tropical Cyclone Olivia over Barrow Island, Australia, in April 1996. It triggered a reading of 408 km/h (253 mph) on an anemometer, which would place it at 17 on the Beaufort scale. Even faster wind speeds may be produced within a tornado.

SOCK TECH

Windsocks, or wind cones, provide a simple indicator of a wind's speed and direction. These textile tubes, commonly seen at airports, lift as wind passes through, turning them in the direction of its motion. The more horizontal and stiff the wind sock appears, the more powerful the wind current. A fully extended windsock may indicate a wind speed of about 28 km/h (17 mph).

▼ *At 10 or above on the Beaufort scale, winds threaten to break or uproot trees, a major hazard for anyone not taking cover.*

BEAUFORT SCALE

NUMBER	DESCRIPTION	WIND SPEED	LAND CONDITIONS
0	CALM	Less than 1 km/h 1 mph	
1	LIGHT AIR	2-5 km/h 1-3 mph	
2	LIGHT BREEZE	6-11 km/h 4-7 mph	
3	GENTLE BREEZE	12-19 km/h 8-12 mph	
4	MODERATE BREEZE	20-28 km/h 13-18 mph	
5	FRESH BREEZE	29-38 km/h 18-23.5 mph	
6	STRONG BREEZE	39-49 km/h 25-31 mph	
7	HIGH WIND, MODERATE GALE	50-61 km/h 32-38 mph	
8	GALE	62-74 km/h 39-46 mph	
9	STRONG OR SEVERE GALE	75-88 km/h 47-54 mph	
10	STORM, WHOLE GALE	89-102 km/h 55-63 mph	
11	VIOLENT STORM	103-117 km/h 64-72 mph	
12	HURRICANE FORCE	More than 118 km/h 73 mph	

▲ *At zero on the Beaufort scale, there is barely a breeze, making sailing using sails almost impossible. Unpowered boats drift with the ocean's current.*

▲ *Trees in a storm can be used as an indicator for Beaufort scale ratings, with a high wind at 7 causing large trees to sway.*

▲ *Gale forces at 8 and above can produce spectacular waves along coasts but life-threatening conditions for anyone in the water.*

OCEAN AND WINDS

Predictable wind patterns and resulting ocean currents have provided ships with fast and reliable sea routes for centuries.

Oceans cover about 70 per cent of our planet and have a huge influence on weather systems. Water warms up and cools down more slowly than land. This makes global temperatures more moderate, preventing the poles from getting too cool and the Equator from becoming too hot. The warmth of the water also affects the temperature of the air above, creating differences in air pressure that trigger winds.

ATMOSPHERIC CELLS

Air circulates above the Earth in a series of looped systems called atmospheric cells – Hadley cells, Ferrel cells and Polar cells. Hadley cells are those created when warm air rises around the Equator, cools in the upper atmosphere and descends in the tropics. The air returning towards the Equator via a Hadley cell is known as a trade wind (see right). Ferrel cells cycle between the tropics and polar regions, while Polar cells bring cool and dry air towards the Equator.

The movement of these winds causes friction on the surface of the oceans, pushing the water at an angle of about 45° from the wind's direction – to the right in the Northern Hemisphere and left in the Southern. The currents are influenced by Earth's rotation as well as the contours of the seafloor and coastlines. Ocean currents are vital for distributing heat and nutrients around the world.

LOCALISED HAZARDS

Sailors use prevailing winds to map their route across the oceans, but they remain at risk from more localised wind patterns. Cyclones and anticyclones (see page 95) can move swiftly across the seas and cause sudden changes in wind direction and strength. Where ocean currents meet land, they can be diverted.

Conversely, where there is no land to act as a break, winds can swell to great speeds, as is the case with the Roaring Forties, strong westerly winds between latitudes 40° and 50° in the Southern Hemisphere.

▼ *Strong currents at sea reach shores as towering waves. Protective seawalls are erected around coastal towns regularly at risk of storms and inland flooding.*

TRADE WINDS

Trade winds are prevailing air currents that continually move from east to west towards the Equator, between belts of calm air and sea known as the horse latitudes. The trade winds meet in a region called the Doldrums where the weather can be extremely calm or highly unpredictable.

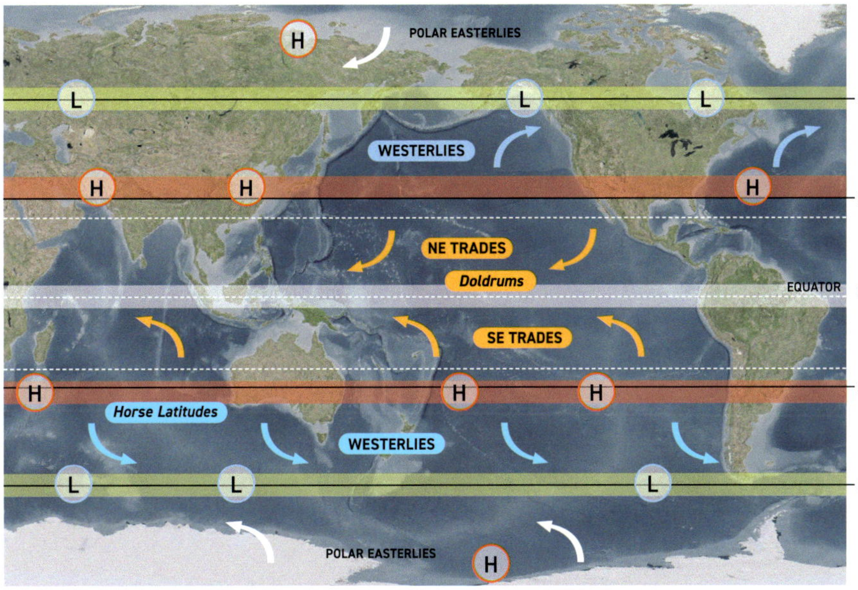

▶ *Prevailing winds blow between distinct latitudes around the world, in generally consistent directions.*

HISTORIC TRADE ROUTES

The trade winds were named for their use by merchant ships crossing the Atlantic and Pacific Oceans. From the 15th century, Portuguese navigators used them to guide their sailing ships from West Africa to the Azores and back to Europe. Trade winds were later used by ships making the voyage from the Americas to Asia. Knowledge of trade winds and other patterns were published in charts from the mid-19th century and have continued to aid sailors looking for a swift passage across the oceans.

▲ *Before the age of steam, sailors relied on trade winds to aid their commercial ocean crossings.*

TROPICAL CYCLONES

The biggest, most violent storms on Earth, tropical cyclones can create gusts over 400 km/h (250 mph) and leave massive devastation in their wakes.

A tropical cyclone is a wide and powerful rotating storm that develops over the South Pacific and Indian oceans. Such storms that originate in the North Atlantic and northeast Pacific are called hurricanes; those from the northwest Pacific are typhoons. They build over warm, tropical seas and, when they reach land, their fierce winds and torrential rain can wreak havoc, ripping up trees and tearing buildings apart.

GAINING STRENGTH

Cyclones typically originate during late summer, over waters with a surface temperature of 27°C (80°F) or above. At this temperature, surface water evaporates quickly, carrying moisture up to 16 km (10 miles) into the troposphere, where it condenses into spinning storm clouds. Cyclones 'feed' on the thermal energy of the water and condensation of water vapour, increasing in strength and size. A typical cyclone will expand to a diameter of 200–500 km (125–310 miles). The largest can reach 1,000 km (620 miles) across. They can last up to three weeks over warm water but will ebb if they pass over land or cooler water where there is less heat and moisture to feed on. Coastlines are most at risk and can face huge storm surges, swells of up to 3 m (10 ft) that hit shore at high speeds.

When winds reach 118 km/h (74 mph), the storm is officially a cyclone and given a name. They are categorised using the Saffir-Simpson scale or similar, from a Category-1 storm, with some flooding and tree damage, to a catastrophic Category 5, with risk to life. Around 80 and 90 cyclones form over tropical waters each year. About 20 of these are Category 3 or higher.

SAFFIR-SIMPSON SCALE

NUMBER	DESCRIPTION	WIND SPEED	LAND CONDITIONS
1	MINIMAL DAMAGE	119-153 km/h 79-95 mph	
2	MODERATE DAMAGE	154-177 km/h 96-110 mph	
3	EXTENSIVE DAMAGE	178-208 km/h 111-129 mph	
4	EXTREME DAMAGE	209-251 km/h 130-156 mph	
5	CATASTROPHIC DAMAGE	> 252+ km/h >157+ mph	

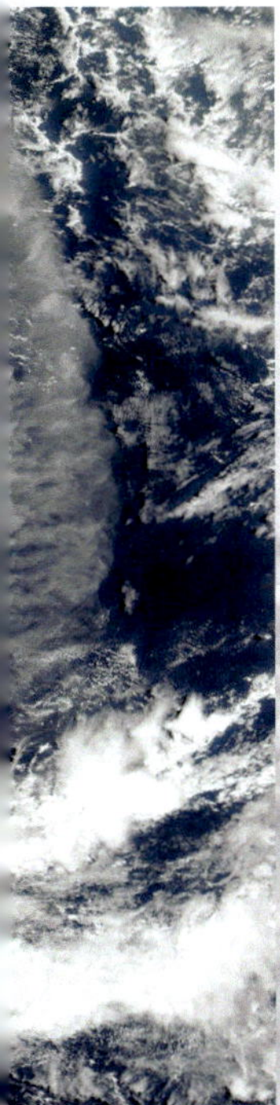

◀ *Satellites track the progress of cyclones, gauging their severity and likelihood of reaching coasts.*

▼ *Air sinks in the centre of a cyclone to form a calm area known as the 'eye', with the strongest winds and heaviest rains building just around it.*

HOW CYCLONES FORM

When water evaporates over warm waters, it rises, condenses and may form tall cumulonimbus thunderclouds several kilometres high. Cool air rushes in to replace the humid air while Earth's rotation makes it spin. This cycle fuels storms that can build into cyclones increasing in size and speed.

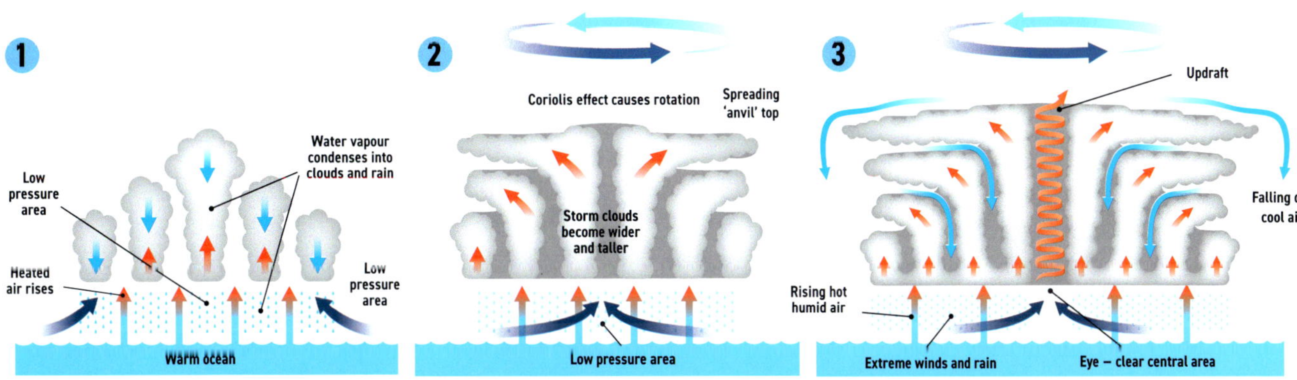

TRACK OF A CYCLONE

Tropical cyclones move away from their origin, pushed by trade winds and ocean currents. In the Atlantic, hurricanes typically track westwards from off the coast of Africa then north or northeast. Their progress is followed by satellites, while brave pilots fly through the storm, avoiding severe vertical winds, to record meteorological data.

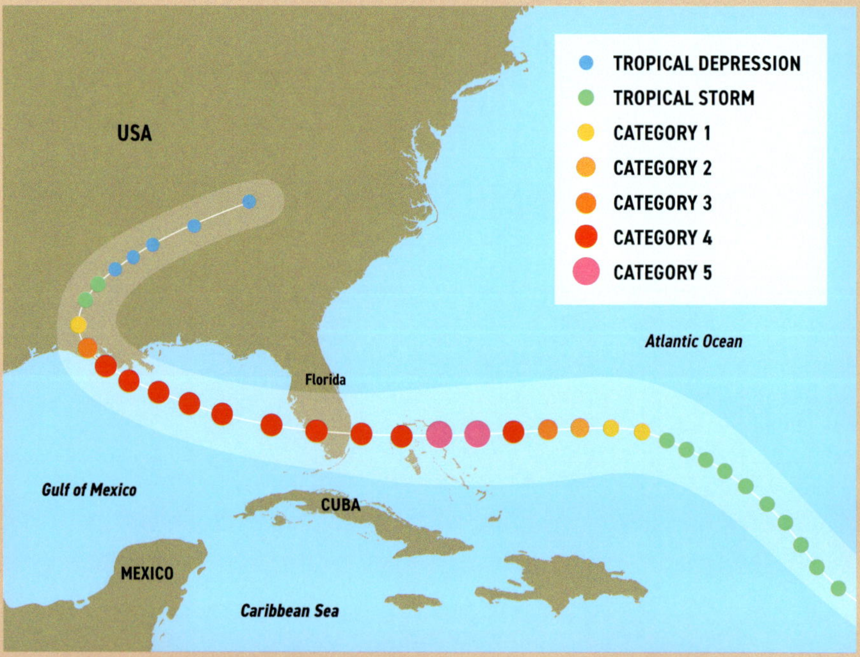

▶ *Modern satellite tracking technology allows authorities to give a clear two-day warning ahead of a tropical cyclone hitting coasts.*

PREPARING FOR THE STORM

Residents on a cyclone's route are encouraged to maintain an emergency rations kit with food, drinking water and a first-aid kit, and to shelter indoors for the duration of the storm. In the most severe circumstances, populations may be evacuated to a safe distance from the storm. The deadliest aspect of a tropical cyclone is not its wind or rain but the flooding caused by a storm surge, especially in low-lying areas. The Category-5 Hurricane Katrina, which hit the southern US in 2005, sent an 8 m (27 ft)-high surge of water 10 km (6 miles) inland. Over 50 levees (embankments), built to keep floods at bay, were inadequate for a surge of this magnitude.

▲ *Ahead of a cyclone's landfall, property owners board up their windows to protect them from flying debris.*

▲ *Storm surges can result in major coastal flooding, many fatalities and hugely expensive repairs to property and infrastructure.*

CYCLONE DAMAGE

Despite modern tracking technology, tropical cyclones may divert unexpectedly and increase in ferocity, leaving communities in their path inadequately prepared for the danger. Thousands of people die every year as the result of these deadly storms. Violent winds can wreck or cause the blockage of roads and bridges, and cut off both power and communications, hampering rescue attempts. Trees and fences fall, and roofs may be torn off buildings. In the aftermath, stagnant water from flooding can lead to the spread of disease. The financial cost of damage to buildings and infrastructure can run into billions of dollars, and it may take years to clear up devastated towns and make repairs.

TORNADOES

Violent funnels of spinning air, tornadoes produce the fastest winds on the planet. They can whip across the land and rip up anything in their paths.

Tornadoes, or twisters, occur almost anywhere in the world, but the majority originate in the Great Plains of North America. The average tornado is short-lived, with a comparatively small diameter of 80 m (260 ft) and a wind speed below 177 km/h (110 mph). The most powerful, though, can grow to 4 km (2.5 miles) across and spin at over 480 km/h (300 mph), the fastest winds recorded on Earth.

INTO THE VORTEX

Tornadoes develop during powerful thunderstorms called supercells. These feature strong, spinning updrafts of air called mesocyclones that may rise for 10 km (6 miles). Cool drafts and rainfall pull these fast-rotating vortexes to the ground to form tornadoes.

The centre of the tornado's spinning vortex is an area of low pressure that can sweep up vehicles and vegetation and tear up buildings that its passes over, transforming the lower parts of the tornado into a murky cloud of soil, dust and debris. The storms may last for minutes or over an hour. The longest-lasting tornado on record was the Tri-State Tornado, which raged for 3.5 hours and travelled at least 352 km (218 miles) across Missouri, Illinois and Indiana in March 1925.

Tornadoes subside when cool winds surround the funnel and cut off the warm air that feeds the storm.

▶ *Where a funnel hits the ground, it pulls buildings apart and tears up the top layers of earth to create a dark swirl of dust and wreckage.*

HOW TORNADOES FORM

Tornadoes form as warm air rises to form towering cumulonimbus thunderclouds. The air within the clouds begins to turn slowly, creating a funnel shape. Cool air pushes this funnel below the cloud. As its diameter shrinks, its spin increases. When the funnel touches the ground, it is a fully formed tornado.

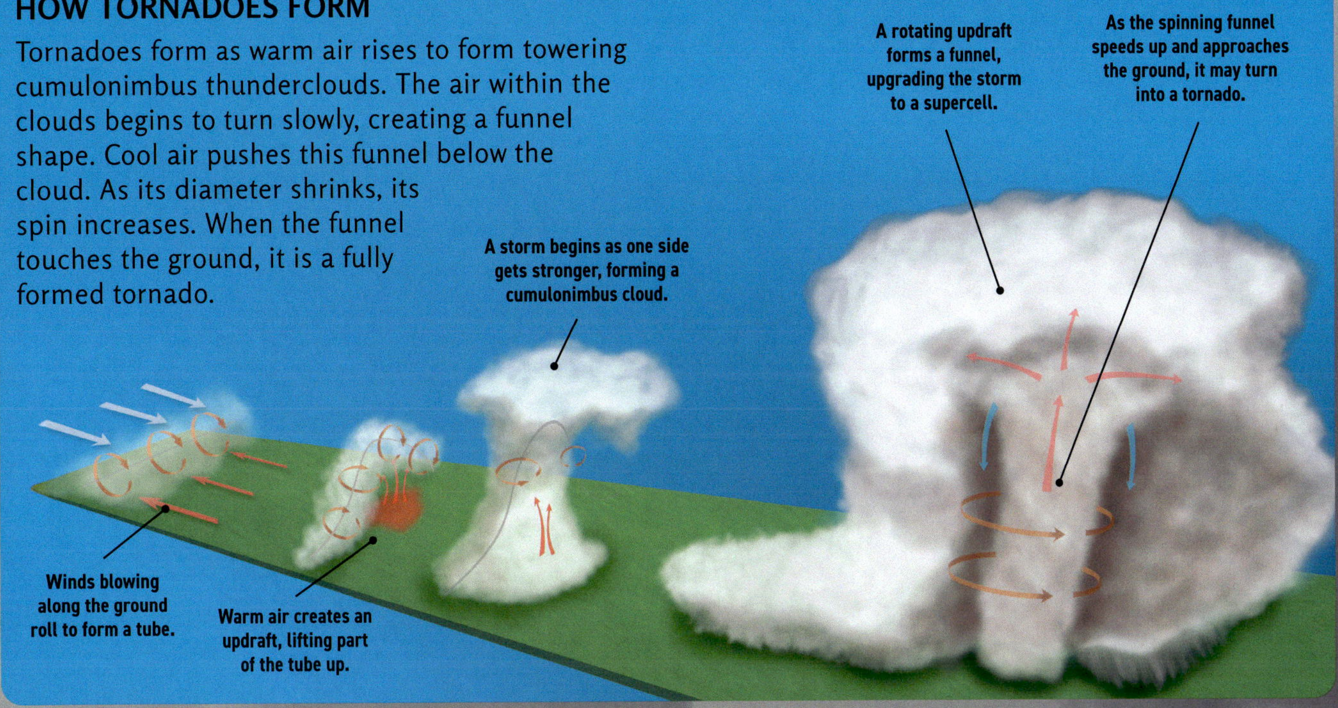

TORNADO ALLEY

Much of central North America is made up of flat grasslands. These Great Plains are notorious for the high number of tornadoes that build up and cross the land, around 1,000 each year, more than anywhere else in the world. In spring, Tornado Alley, as it is known, receives cold air from Canada and the Rocky Mountains and warm moist air from the Gulf of Mexico. The combination provides the ideal circumstances for thunderstorms to form.

▼ *The meeting of cold northern air, dry desert air and humid air from the south creates conditions for intense storms in the US's Tornado Alley.*

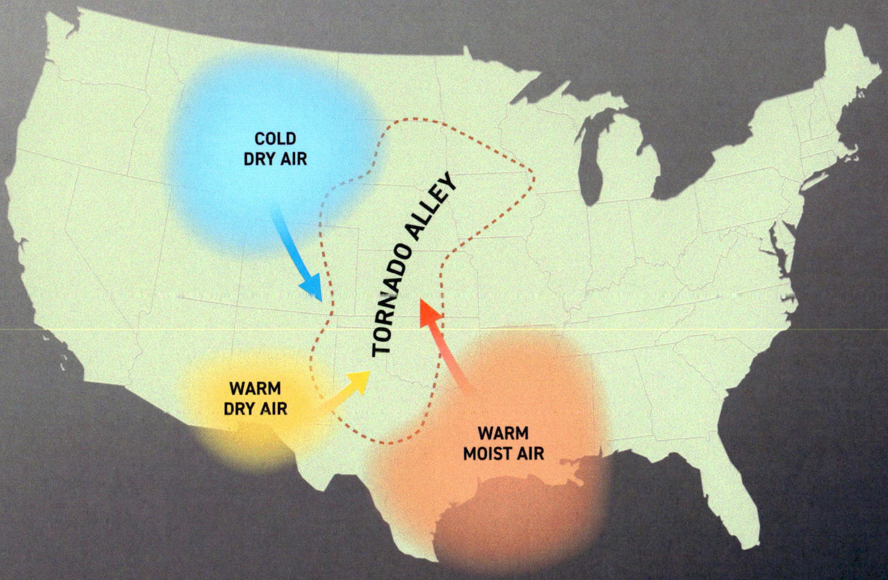

SUPERCELL TO TWISTER

Around 30 per cent of supercell storms will give rise to tornadoes. Some tell-tale signs that one could form include the appearance of a wall cloud – an isolated, lowering band of cloud. Some also develop circular bands called a collar cloud, which is created by extremely strong updrafts from the wall cloud below. Striations in the clouds also indicate that they are rotating fast and strong. A horseshoe-shaped 'clear slot' in the supercell is where a twister is most likely to form.

▲ *Derechos are wide-spreading, heavy windstorms that appear during warmer months and may last for days.*

DERECHO DANGER

No less dangerous than tornadoes are storms called derechos, rare but long-lasting tempests that leave a trail of damage at least 400 km (250 miles) in length. These are also formed from thunderstorms, when a continuous narrow band of storms mass ahead of a cold front. A sign of an impending derecho is a threatening wedge of low, dark clouds, called an arcus.

Derechos can produce straight-line gusts close to tornado speed and cause immense damage through violent downward bursts of air and rain. They are extremely hazardous for aircraft due to their powerful downbursts and upbursts, while being hard to dodge due to their vast width.

STORM CHASERS

Despite the danger, some people actively chase tornadoes, to study the storms or enjoy the thrill of being close to such a powerful force of nature. For safety, storm chasers drive heavy, armoured vehicles with equipment that can monitor weather patterns and signs of impending tornadoes. They must be alert for debris on the road, position themselves away from a tornado's forward path and have an escape route planned.

▶ *Undeterred by the risks of getting close to tornadoes, storm chasers track, observe and record these fearsome storms.*

▼ *From above, the trail of damage left by a tornado is clear, with homes ripped apart and the debris scattered along a wide path.*

FUJITA SCALE

Tornadoes are measured not just by their wind speed but for the damage they leave in their wake. The Enhanced Fujita scale records damage to buildings and vegetation to provide a rating from 0 for light damage to 5 for the most ferocious of storms.

SCALE	WINDSPEED	FREQUENCY	INFORMATION
EFU	N/A	3.11%	**No observable damage**
EF0	65-85 mph / 105-137 km/h	52.82%	**Minor damage:** Some light roof and tree damage
EF1	86-110 mph / 138-177 km/h	32.98%	**Moderate damage:** Broken windows, roof and door damage
EF2	111-135 mph / 178-217 km/h	8.41%	**Significant damage:** Roofs torn off, cars and mobile homes tossed, trees snapped and uprooted
EF3	136-165 mph / 218-266 km/h	2.18%	**Severe damage:** Significant damage to buildings, including losing whole stories or houses with weak foundations being blown away
EF4	166-200 mph / 267-322 km/h	0.46%	**Devastating damage:** Well-constructed home levelled; brick walls collapse; vehicles thrown significant distances
EF5	>200 mph / 322 km/h	0.05%	**Incredible damage:** Severe structural damage, even to reinforced concrete buildings; trees debarked and snapped

TRACKING TORNADOES

Tornadoes, along with cyclones and derechos, can be monitored using orbital weather satellites while sophisticated ground-based Doppler radar systems can detect the velocity and direction of storms, so their potential to become tornadoes can be assessed. When there is a high risk of tornadoes developing within hours, a tornado watch is issued. Trained storm spotters are employed to report sightings to national weather services who can then broadcast public alerts. When a tornado is confirmed, a warning is issued online and over radio and TV, and anyone in the tornado's path is advised to seek shelter. In some Tornado Alley states, alarms are fitted onto towers.

▼ *Weather satellites continually monitor weather patterns from orbit for meteorologists to interpret.*

DUST STORMS

These kilometre-high walls of dust and sand driven by winds can block out the Sun and bury towns, causing disruption and laying waste to farmland.

Heat and lack of water are not the only perils for those living in and around deserts and other arid lands. When updrafts of warm air rise by convection, cool air rushes in from either side to replace it. This draft can lift the loose and light sand and soils from the ground, forming a dust storm, a dense cloud that can travel for thousands of kilometres and blot out the Sun.

DESERT TRAILS

When the winds that blow across North Africa's Sahara, Mongolia's Gobi Desert, West Asia's Arabian Desert and India's Thar Desert reach speeds of 24 km/h (15 mph), they are strong enough to lift fine grains more than a metre. The largest of these wind storms can develop into walls of dust up to 1.5 km (1 mile) high. When these blow in, visibility is severely reduced, the air becomes dangerous to breathe in and travel becomes impossible. As the dust rushes across the land, it can leave buildings, roads and railway tracks buried.

The dust lifted during such huge storms may drift in the upper atmosphere and fall thousands of kilometres away, leaving trails of powder in cities far beyond the deserts. Sand transported through the air from the Sahara has even been detected in the Amazon rainforest and western Atlantic Ocean. This spread of dust across the globe can be beneficial, delivering nutrients that fertilise lands and oceans.

FARMS RAVAGED

The impact of dust storms can be aggravated by dry weather and poor farming practices, such as uprooting vegetation, exposing the soil to winds. In areas like North America's

▲ *Rusty sand lifted from Australia's Outback during a 2009 dust storm fills the air to cast an orange filter over Sydney's Harbour Bridge.*

Great Plains, dust storms can remove the top soil from agricultural land and leave farms unable to plant crops. In the 1930s, drought and severe dust storms caused major hardship for farmers in the prairies of Canada and the United States during a period known as the Dust Bowl.

DUST DEVILS

Unlike larger wind funnels, such as tornadoes, dust devils are not the result of thunderclouds. They emerge during hot weather over dry ground, when upward currents of warm air called thermals begin spinning and lift dust from the ground. At times these can become large and strong enough to bring down power lines.

◀ *A dust storm, or haboob, forms when cold air from a thunderstorm rushes downwards. Here, a haboob fills the horizon in the Sonoran Desert in Arizona, USA.*

EXTREME WIND EVENTS

Tornadoes, cyclones and dust storms have resulted in huge destruction and loss of life, even as early warning systems have become more advanced.

Though we know much more about how wind storms develop, and have sophisticated satellite and ground warning systems in place, climate change looks likely to increase the unpredictability and severity of storms, and direct them into regions unprepared for such events. As these examples of extreme disasters attest, we remain at the mercy of the weather.

Black Sunday dust storm
USA, 1935

The 1930s brought great hardship to farmers living on the North American Great Plains. During an eight-year drought known as the Dust Bowl, one of the worst wind storms on record kicked off on 14 April 1935, when millions of tonnes of dirt blew through at 100 km/h (60 mph), producing darkness in the daytime.

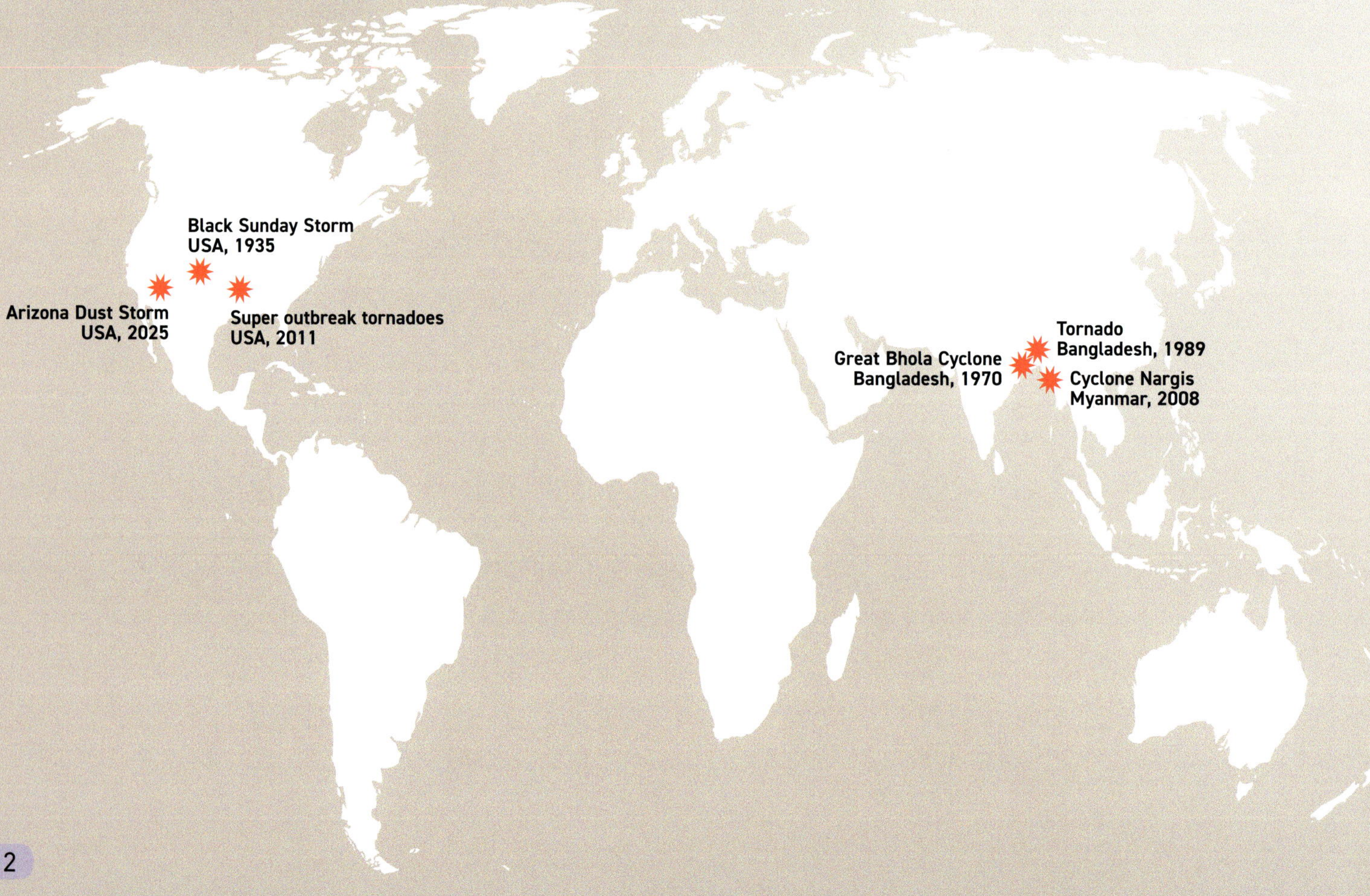

Deadliest tornado
Bangladesh, 1989

Considered the deadliest tornado in history, the storm that hit the Manikganj district of Bangladesh on 26 April 1989 was about 1.6 km (1 mile) wide and destroyed every building within 6 sq km (2.5 sq miles). Around 1,300 people were killed, thousands injured and tens of thousands left homeless.

Cyclone Nargis
Myanmar, 2008

Nargis, a Category-4 tropical cyclone tore through central Myanmar on 2 May 2008, causing a storm surge 3.7 m (12 ft) high. With no warning system, evacuation plans or shelters in place, an estimated 140,000 people were killed.

Arizona dust storm
USA, 2025

Phoenix, Arizona, USA, was plunged into darkness on 25 August 2025 when a mammoth dust storm, known as a haboob, engulfed the city. The storm was followed by a series of severe thunderstorms and 113 km/h (70 mph) wind gusts that toppled trees and caused power outages.

Great Bhola Cyclone
Bangladesh, 1970

The deadliest tropical cyclone on record hit what would become Bangladesh on 12 November 1970. The floods from the resulting 10 m (33 ft)-high storm surge over the low-lying and densely populated Bay of Bengal caused up to half a million fatalities and 86 million dollars of damage.

Super outbreak tornadoes
USA, 2011

During 2011, the US saw the largest number of tornadoes rage across 21 states. In what was called a Super Outbreak, over 200 tornadoes were recorded in just four days in April, including four given the highest rating on the Fujita scale. Despite early warnings, 319 people lost their lives.

5 EXTREME WATER

WHY DOES IT RAIN?

Rain is essential for life. It delivers fresh water for drinking, cleaning, growing crops and generating electricity, thanks to a natural recycling process.

Water exists on Earth as a liquid, ice and vapour and is endlessly recycled and cleaned through a process known as the hydrologic or water cycle. This cycle brings us rain – a type of precipitation – along with sleet, snow and hail. Some rain is collected in lakes and reservoirs; some seeps into the earth as groundwater. Some flows along rivers to seas and oceans.

THE WATER CYCLE

When the temperature rises, more evaporation occurs. This is a process where liquid water turns into a gas called water vapour. The vapour rises until it reaches a height where the air is cooler. Here it goes through a process called condensation in which the vapour forms tiny water droplets around minuscule particles, such as dust, salt or pollen. These droplets are light enough to float in the air. Grouped together they form clouds. As seas and oceans cover much of the planet,

▶ *The hydrologic cycle is a continuous movement of Earth's water through evaporation from liquid to vapour, then condensation into clouds before falling as precipitation.*

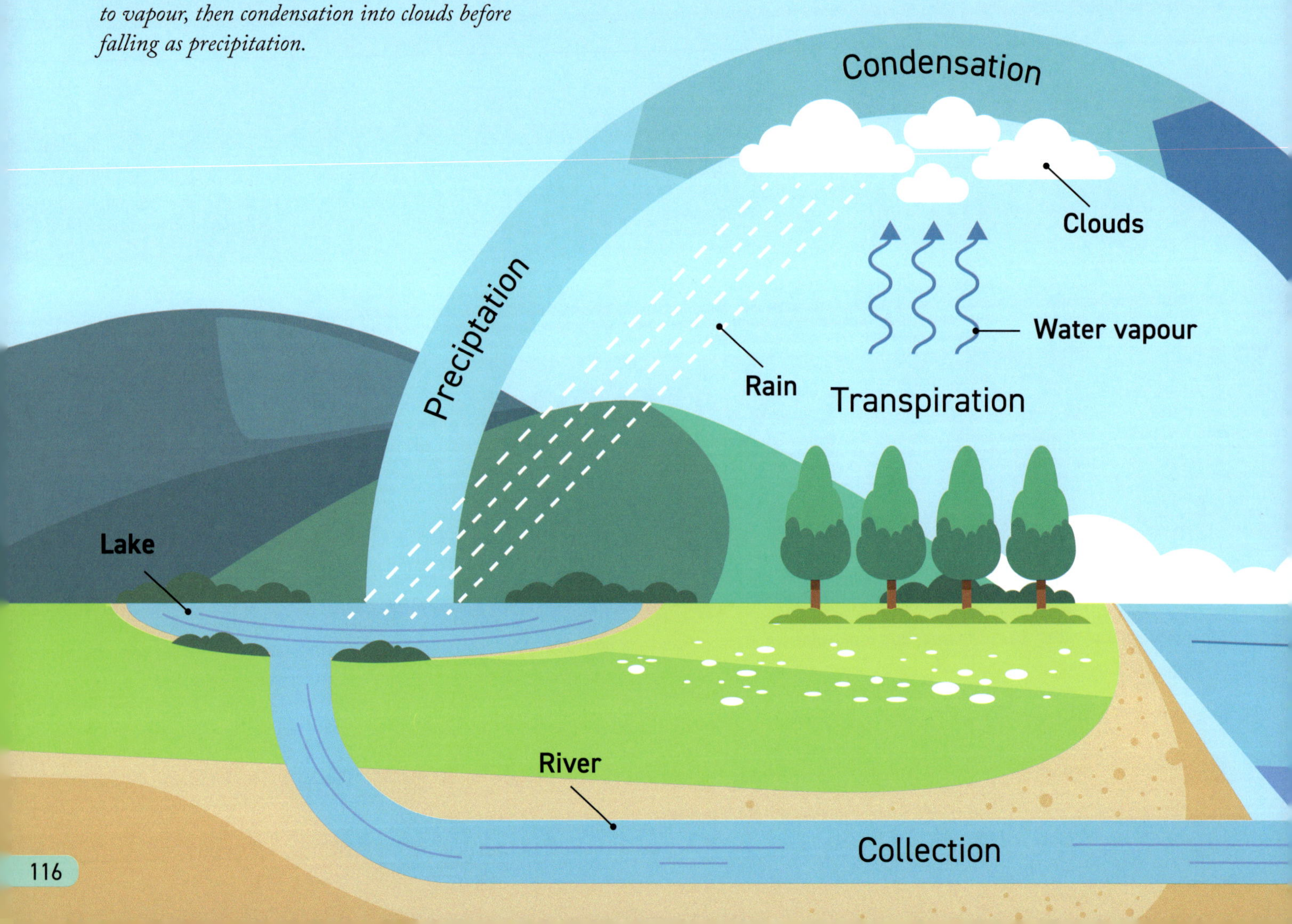

more than 80 per cent of evaporation takes place over large bodies of saltwater. Water vapour also rises from freshwater lakes and rivers, and from plants through transpiration, evaporating through minute pores called stomata on their leaves.

The clouds are transported around the world by wind. When most of a cloud warms to above freezing, the water droplets begin to fall or be blown about through the cloud, combining with others until they become too heavy to float, and they fall as rain.

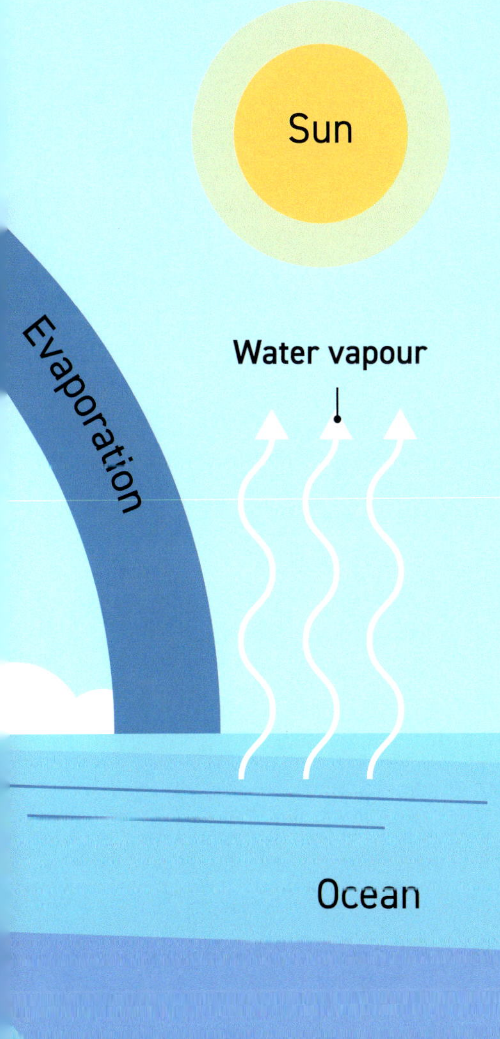

TYPES OF RAIN

Rainfall is unequal across the planet. In parts of Antarctica, the temperature is too low for rain, while deserts are too hot and dry for clouds to form. The heaviest rains occur in tropical and temperate regions, with much falling over rainforests. Rainfall is also affected by the landscape, where weather fronts meet coastlines or mountains. Rains brought about by particular geographical formations or circumstances have specific names.

RELIEF RAIN

When air moves up the side of a peak to cooler heights, it condenses to produce rain, which falls mostly on that side. Once the air passes over the peak, it descends and warms up, resulting in drier conditions known as a rain shadow.

CONVECTIONAL RAIN

Convectional rain occurs when the Sun heats the land, warming the air above it. The warm, moist air rises quickly, then cools to form clouds. Convectional rain is most common in tropical regions and during the summer months.

FRONTAL RAIN

When a warm-weather front (area of high pressure) meets a cold front (area of low pressure), the cold air sinks and the warm air rises to form clouds that may deliver heavy rain.

CLOUDS

Clouds come in many forms and at different levels in the atmosphere. Their shape and hue can provide an indication of the weather ahead.

Clouds build in the troposphere, the lowest layer in Earth's atmosphere, where almost all the moisture is held. They usually appear white as they scatter all the light that hits them in all directions, but rain clouds can appear grey from underneath. Clouds are divided into three main groups, each with a descriptive Latin name: cirrus means 'curl', stratus means 'layer', and cumulus 'heap'. They are also classified according to the type of weather they bring and how high they appear in the atmosphere. Stratus is a low-lying cloud (below 2 km/1.2 miles), while those with 'alto' in the name are at medium heights (2–7 km/1.2–4.3 miles). Those at higher and colder levels tend to be formed of ice crystals rather than liquid droplets.

CIRROSTRATUS
Found in the cold upper troposphere, above 6 km (4 miles), cirrostratus clouds are made up of tiny ice crystals. Though they may be hundreds of metres thick, these clouds appear as wispy, transparent sheets. The light of the Sun or Moon may create a halo in them.

ALTOCUMULUS
Altocumulus are mid-level clouds made up of both water and ice. They form in bunched-up rows like strings of cotton-wool balls. The rounded white and grey clumps are called cloudlets. Altocumulus appear with settled weather, rarely bringing rain on their own.

ALTOSTRATUS
Like altocumulus, altostratus are mid-level clouds, found between 2 and 6 km (1.2 and 4 miles) up. The clouds appear as flattened streaks across the sky and evolve from descending cirrostratus clouds. Altostratus clouds usually appear ahead of lower-lying clouds, such as nimbostratus, that bring rain.

CIRROCUMULUS
Cirrocumulus are found at higher levels as mats of cloudlets or rippled sheets. Sometimes they produce a fish-scale pattern, known as a 'mackerel sky'. Mostly made of ice crystals, cirrocumulus clouds rarely deliver rain and do not last for long.

CIRRUS

These high white clouds appear as curls or filaments, the result of their ice crystals being strung out by drafts of wind. Cirrus clouds can be formed from contrails, the vapours left behind by aircraft. They indicate fine weather but can precede rainier clouds.

CUMULONIMBUS

Cumulonimbus is the archetypal thundercloud, towering sometimes up to 16 km (10 miles) – the whole height of the troposphere – and flattened on top, like an anvil. They can bring heavy rain, hail, thunder and lightning, and can even develop into a tornado.

CUMULUS

Cumulus are the white fluffy clouds with distinct shapes that most match children's drawings of the sky. These low-level clouds build separately rather than grouping into sheets and are short-lived, lasting less than an hour. They typically appear during periods of fine weather.

NIMBOSTRATUS

Nimbo means 'bearing rain'. This mid-level featureless cloud is dense and dark, blocking out sunlight and often blanketing most of the sky. Nimbostratus clouds hover below higher clouds, bringing persistent wet weather that can last for hours, or snow when it's cold.

STRATOCUMULUS

Stratocumulus are low-level clouds that form in rounded clumps. They're often stratus clouds that have spread out and arranged in bands with space between them. Stratocumulus are common over seas and may appear ahead of a cold or warm front, indicating weather shifts.

STRATUS

Stratus are indistinct, low-lying clouds that form sheets or layers, grey or white in colour. They sometimes linger close to the ground, forming mist or fog. Of the little rain produced by stratus clouds, most falls as light drizzle or snow.

ACID RAIN

The burning of fossil fuels can adversely affect the acidity of rain, causing erosion on buildings and environmental disaster.

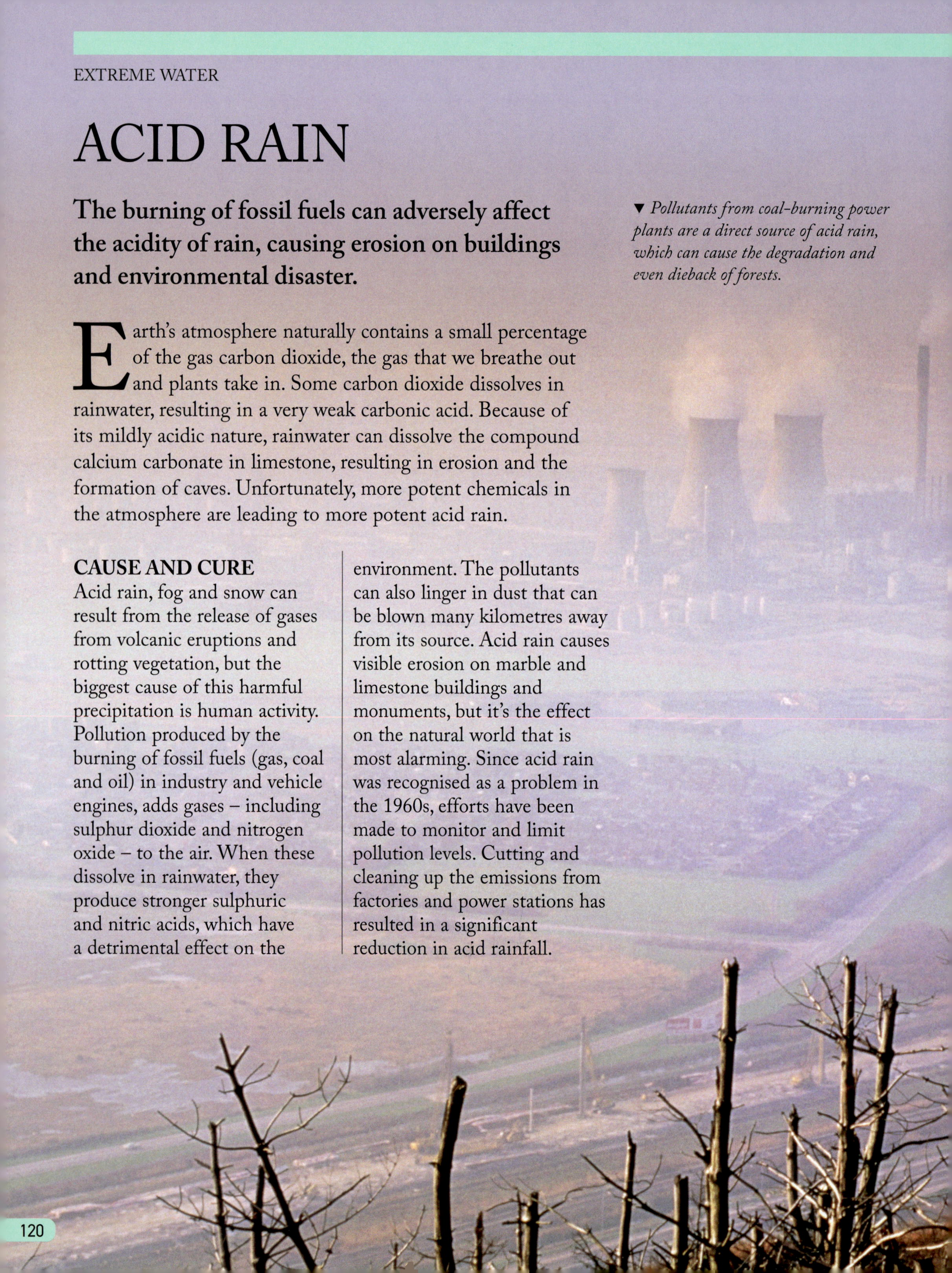

▼ *Pollutants from coal-burning power plants are a direct source of acid rain, which can cause the degradation and even dieback of forests.*

Earth's atmosphere naturally contains a small percentage of the gas carbon dioxide, the gas that we breathe out and plants take in. Some carbon dioxide dissolves in rainwater, resulting in a very weak carbonic acid. Because of its mildly acidic nature, rainwater can dissolve the compound calcium carbonate in limestone, resulting in erosion and the formation of caves. Unfortunately, more potent chemicals in the atmosphere are leading to more potent acid rain.

CAUSE AND CURE

Acid rain, fog and snow can result from the release of gases from volcanic eruptions and rotting vegetation, but the biggest cause of this harmful precipitation is human activity. Pollution produced by the burning of fossil fuels (gas, coal and oil) in industry and vehicle engines, adds gases – including sulphur dioxide and nitrogen oxide – to the air. When these dissolve in rainwater, they produce stronger sulphuric and nitric acids, which have a detrimental effect on the environment. The pollutants can also linger in dust that can be blown many kilometres away from its source. Acid rain causes visible erosion on marble and limestone buildings and monuments, but it's the effect on the natural world that is most alarming. Since acid rain was recognised as a problem in the 1960s, efforts have been made to monitor and limit pollution levels. Cutting and cleaning up the emissions from factories and power stations has resulted in a significant reduction in acid rainfall.

EFFECTS ON THE NATURAL WORLD

Acid rain burns the leaves on plants and removes nutrients, such as calcium, from the soil that plants need for growth. It also frees aluminium in the dirt, which, once dissolved, suppresses a plant's ability to absorb water. The result is stressed and unhealthy vegetation, and even the death of forests, particularly those at high altitudes. Acidic precipitation enters lakes and streams, resulting in greater aluminium absorption from soils. This can turn surface waters toxic for some wildlife and damage fish gills. Calcium levels are reduced, affecting the ability of molluscs, such as snails, to grow their shells.

▶ *Acid rain can weaken the ability of trees to survive droughts, severe weather, pests and disease.*

WHY DOES IT HAPPEN?

Emissions from power plants, factories and motor vehicles add sulphur dioxide (SO_2) and nitrogen oxide (NO) to the air. These react with water and oxygen in the atmosphere to form mild sulphuric and nitric acids, a process sped up by sunlight. The acids mix with rain and dust and are transported around the planet by winds. When they fall to the ground, they can adversely affect plant and animal life.

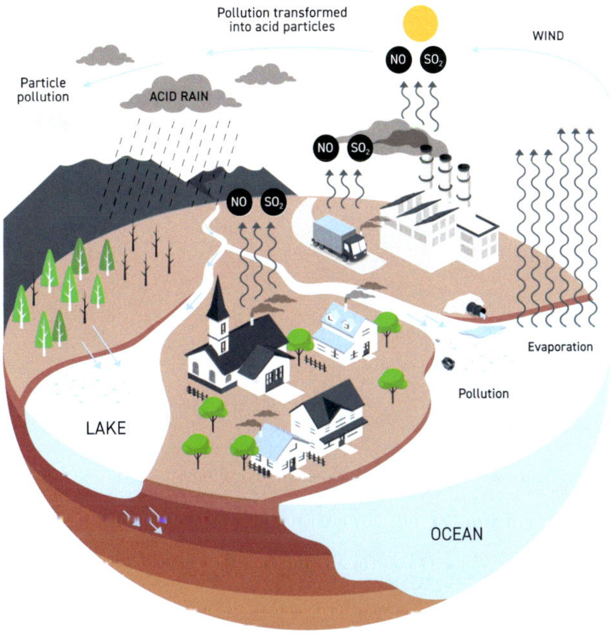

SUPERCELL STORMS

The rarest and most severe thunderstorms, supercells have a rotating updraft (rising current of air) that can make them rage for hours. In the process, they can produce torrential downpours of rain and hail. Supercells occur more frequently in areas like Colorado's eastern plains (pictured) where warm, moist air regularly meets cooler, dry air, causing instability.

MONSOON

Monsoons are seasonal winds that bring months of dry weather followed by heavy downpours. These contrasting conditions create major challenges.

The word 'monsoon' derives from the Arabic word for season and describes changes in wind direction through the tropics. For the Indian Subcontinent, winter winds blow in from Central Asia and lose moisture as they pass the Himalayas. This results in six months of dry weather. In summer, as a low-pressure system develops over the surrounding highlands, the winds switch direction from northeast to southeast, drawing moist air from the Indian Ocean and delivering heavy downpours.

▲ *In the months leading up to the monsoon rains, rivers and reservoirs may run dry.*

The difference in rainfall between the winter and summer monsoons is extreme. Mumbai in India typically receives just 100 mm (4 in) of rain between October and May compared to 1,700 mm (67 in) from June to October. Temperatures during the dry season can rise to 50°C (122°F) in South Asia.

The arrival of the summer rains comes as a relief after months of hot, dry weather and an oppressively humid spring. Farms rely on the rain's timely arrival in the summer, for crops and animals. Hydroelectric power plants across India and Southeast Asia also depend on the summer rains.

The summer monsoon generally begins with thunderstorms and torrential rain that can last for weeks and cause major flooding. The rainfall progresses northwards through June and July, coming to a halt at the Himalayas.

Monsoons are not only a weather feature for the Indian Subcontinent and southeast Asia. Less extreme monsoon rains affect parts of Australia, Africa and the Americas.

PUBLIC TRANSPORT

Flooding is common during the first weeks of the monsoon rains. The Indian metropolis of Mumbai faces annual deluges with up to 0.5 m (1.5 ft) of water covering the streets and pouring into its underground metro system. The waters can cause roads to collapse and bring traffic to a halt. In more rural areas, the heavy rains carry the risk of mudslides.

▲ *Monsoon downpours can flood railway stations in tropical countries, such as Indonesia, and require emergency evacuations.*

▼ *People living in the range of monsoons are used to the extreme weather conditions, and continue fishing and farming even under heavy downpours.*

DEWATERING PUMPS

Cities affected by monsoon rains may struggle to cope due to insufficient drainage, both human-made or via naturally occurring rivers and wetlands. Pumps – such as the one seen below, in Thailand after Typhoon Tien Mu in 2021 – are needed to remove the rainfall that floods into basements, subways and mines. It may take months, even years, to repair damage and dry off submerged infrastructure.

FLOODS

Floods are by far the most serious natural disasters, responsible for more deaths, injuries and costly property damage than any other weather phenomena.

Floods are often due to a major storm and heavier-than-expected rains. Climate change has made flooding more common, as melting ice at the poles raises sea levels and changing weather patterns push stormy weather to areas unprepared for surges. Progressive river floods can lead to costly property damage and evacuations while flash floods threaten life with fast-moving waves of water that engulf neighbourhoods.

DEADLY DELUGE

Most rainfall or melting snow drains away, soaking into the ground, flowing seaward along rivers or feeding into drainage systems. But in extreme circumstances, surface waters build up, rivers and drains overflow, and waters cover the land and pour into buildings, causing massive disruption.

Most flooding is gradual. These river floods allow time for people to move belongings and escape waterlogged areas. In extreme weather, dams or riverbanks may be breached and sudden rushes of water may pour out, while in the worst circumstances, flash floods occur, hitting populated areas like a mini-tsunami.

The worst natural disaster in the last century was the flooding of China's Yangtze River in 1931, which was responsible for over three million deaths.

▲ *Gauges indicate water levels along flood-prone rivers. Records of water levels date back centuries.*

▼ *Floods in Pakistan occur repeatedly due to monsoon rains and rivers overflowing, with water-covered fields stretching to the horizon.*

RISING SEA LEVELS

Over the last 150 years, sea levels have been rising by an average of 21–24 cm (8–9 in) and at increasing speed during the 21st century. This acceleration is likely due to the effects of global warming, with ice sheets and glaciers melting and warmer seas expanding. Higher tides, coastal erosion and more unpredictable weather patterns leave people living along coasts at greater risk of flooding while low-lying islands face complete submersion.

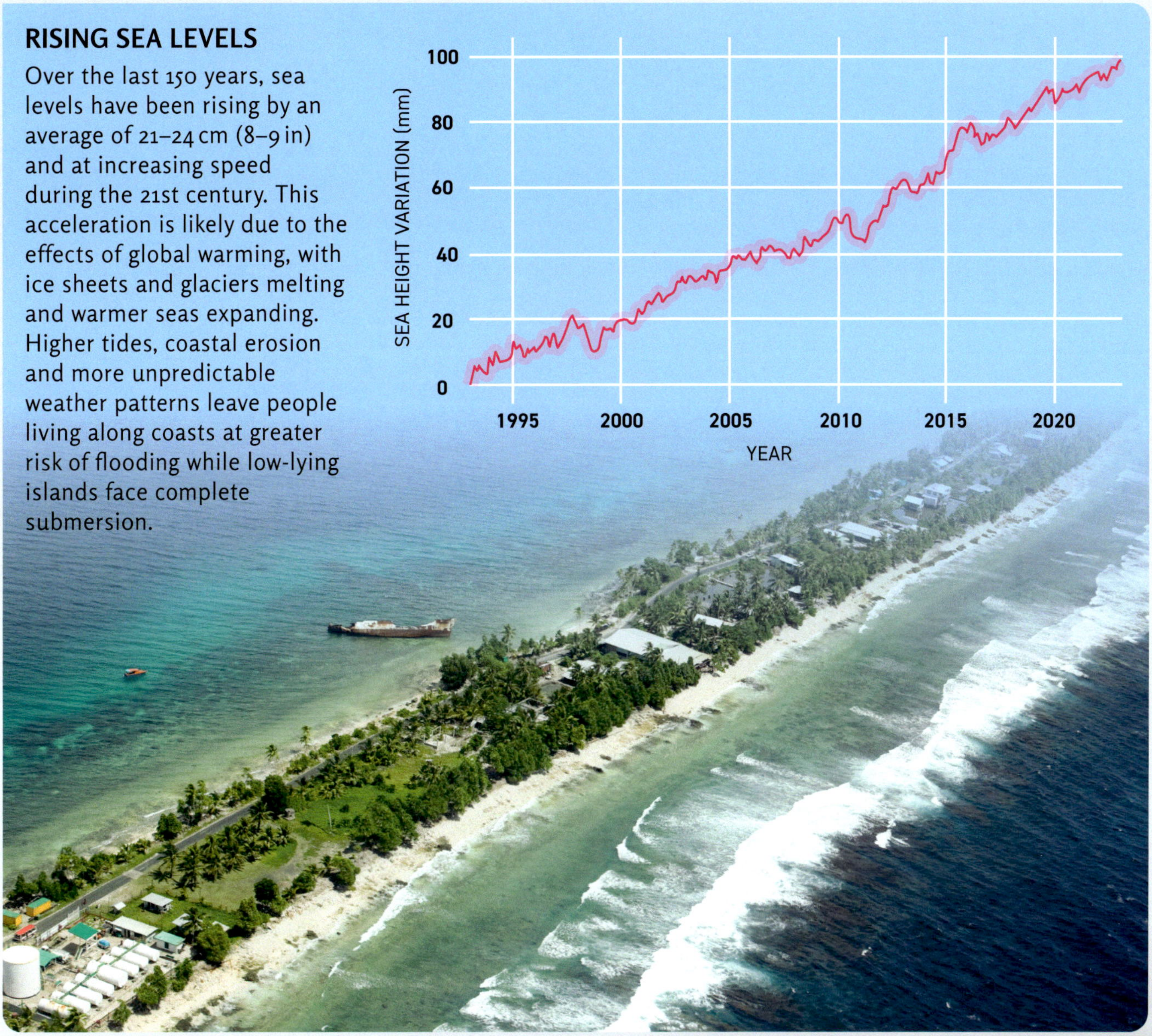

FIGHTING FLOODS

Water level monitoring and computer models can help predict flooding so emergency measures can be put in place. Where river levels regularly swell, high banks, dams or levees can be built. The best means of flood control are natural routes for rainwaters to flow, along rivers or to wetlands and floodplains, where the water can slowly drain away.

Unfortunately, with rising populations, more land is being given over to construction, reducing the areas where rainwater can seep into soils.

▲ *Temporary flood measures, such as sandbags and covered metal frames, are put in place when river levels threaten to rise higher than permanent barriers.*

CAUGHT IN A FLASH

Flash floods can occur without warning, with water levels rising by a metre in minutes, causing torrents to pour down streets, tossing vehicles aside and submerging the floors of buildings. These sudden floods, caused by severe storms, meltwater from ice and snow or the bursting of dams, are particularly dangerous in mountainous areas, where heavy downpours may be channelled at speed towards valleys. A 1979 flash flood in Gujarat, India (below), caused up to 25,000 deaths, while flash floods in Valencia, Spain, in 2024 (right) were some of the worst (and most expensive) natural disasters in Europe.

▼ *Vehicles can be swept away by the force of a flash flood. Attempts to drive through even shallow moving waters present significant risk.*

THAMES BARRIER

One of the largest moveable flood barriers in the world, the Thames Barrier began operating in 1983 to prevent the tidal waters of the River Thames spilling over banks in central London upstream. The barrier features ten five-storey-high steel gates, each weighing 3,300 tonnes (3,600 tons). Since its opening, the barrier has needed to close more than 200 times as a flood defence.

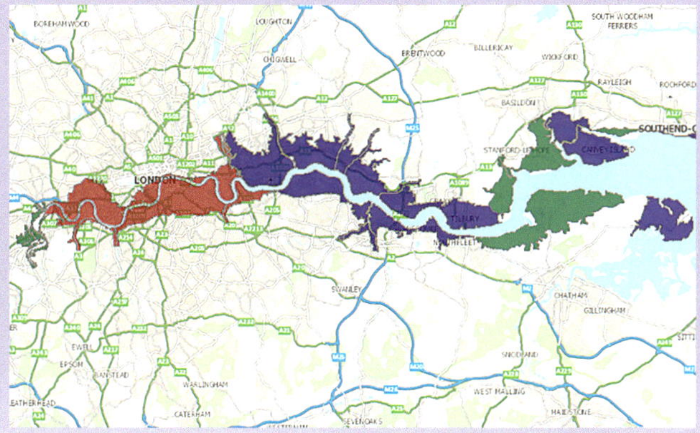

▼ *To cope with rising sea levels, the Thames Barrier gates may need to be raised by another 50 cm (20 in) before the end of the century.*

▲ *Stretching across Brazil, Paraguay and Bolivia, the Pantanal floodplain becomes the world's largest tropical freshwater wetland during the rainy season.*

FERTILE FLOODPLAINS

Floodplains are low-lying landscapes beside rivers where flooding regularly occurs. The river, or floodway, can be dry for part of the year but during wet seasons, waters can spread out for thousands of kilometres, to form wetland environments. Wetlands provide important habitats for numerous rare species.

Due to the predictability of the floods' rising waters and nutrient-rich sediments, floodplains also attract farmers. Ancient Egypt, for example, flourished for centuries thanks to the high-yielding Nile floodplains, while today, Argentina's pampas are ideal for cereal crops and cattle.

TYPHOON FLOODING

This aerial shot of a town built along a river basin in Thailand shows houses and buildings submerged in floodwaters following a 2022 typhoon. The floods spanned 33 provinces, affecting more than 87,000 households. Heavy rains wash mud, soil and vegetation from the land into the water, making floodwaters appear a tea-like brown. When floods hit during monsoon season, it can take days or even months for floodwaters to recede due to the persistent rain.

STORM SURGES

A terrifyingly tall wave of water crashing over sea walls, a storm surge can destroy boats and buildings, erode beaches and damage coastal habitats.

A dangerously large increase in sea level, a storm surge can submerge coastal communities. In a storm, gale-force winds push water towards the land. Combined with low air pressure allowing the water to bulge up and Earth's natural rotation, water is forced upwards to create a storm surge. When land is only slightly higher than sea level, or in some places even lower and protected by barriers, it can quickly become flooded.

WEATHER THE STORM

The highest rises in sea level often occur during tropical cyclones. These intense storms, also called typhoons and hurricanes, feature powerful winds, and the sea level rises where these winds are strongest. Storm surges resulting from tropical cyclones can reach up to 10 m (33 ft) tall. In a cooler, temperate region, such as most of Europe, storm surges don't usually exceed 3 m (10 ft).

A negative storm surge sees water being blown away from

▲ *The defence walls around New Orleans, USA, provided little protection against Hurricane Katrina's storm surge in 2005. This barge was pushed up against flooded homes by huge waves.*

the coastline and the sea dropping below its normal levels. It can leave ships damaged or stranded and the exposed seabed is dangerous because water levels can quickly rise again when the wind conditions change.

SURGE PROTECTORS

In some places, sea defences are built to minimise the dangers of storm surges. After extensive flooding in 1953, the Thames Barrier was constructed to protect London from the effects of future tidal surges in the North Sea. Computer programmes are also used by scientists to predict storm surges. In the US, the National Weather Service uses a system called SLOSH – Sea, Lake and Overland Surges from Hurricanes.

TIDE GUIDE

The height of a storm surge depends on several elements. It will increase if it occurs at the same time as the high tide. The slope of the ocean floor also plays a part. A gradual slope tends to produce a higher storm surge than a steep one.

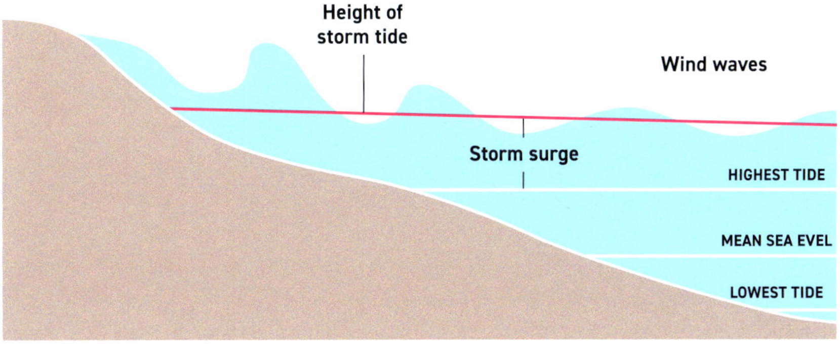

▼ *Winthrop Beach in Massachusetts, USA, was battered by storm surges in 2013. It was the result of Winter Storm Nemo, which caused blizzard conditions and flooding.*

ROGUE WAVES

Once believed to be no more than a scary legend from seafarers' stories, rogue waves are real – and powerful enough to crack a ship's hull.

For hundreds of years, most people thought tales of rogue waves were exaggerated. It wasn't until the late 20th century that one was finally measured off the coast of Norway. Also called monster waves and extreme storm waves, a rogue wave is an unexpectedly high wall of water. It must be at least twice the height of the significant wave height, which is the average height of the tallest third of waves around it.

MARITIME MENACE

It's believed that rogue waves are responsible for several ships' damage or disappearance. In July 1909, the SS *Waratah* vanished on its voyage to South Africa, and some experts think an extreme storm wave was the cause. In 1975, the 222 m-long (728 ft-long) SS *Edmund Fitzgerald* rapidly sank in a storm, perhaps due to a monster wave breaking it apart. The large freighter was lost on Lake Superior in North America; rogue waves can form in fresh water as well as oceans.

Although they occur worldwide, scientists are not certain how often rogue waves happen. Now it is recognised they do exist, sensors attached to floating buoys are being used to record them. The biggest rogue wave, in relation to significant wave height, was registered by a buoy in November 2020 in the North Pacific Ocean. At 17.6 m (57.7 ft) – the height of a five-storey building, it was almost three times taller than nearby waves.

▲ *In* The Great Wave Off Kanagawa, *a famous 19th-century print by artist Katsushika Hokusai, fishermen are threatened by a rogue wave.*

THE DRAUPNER WAVE

The first rogue wave to be recorded was on New Year's Day in 1995. A massive wave hit the Draupner E oil-drilling platform in the North Sea. A laser gauge measured its height at 25.6 m (84 ft), shown by the distance between the peak and the trough on the chart. This was twice the height of the waves immediately before and after it.

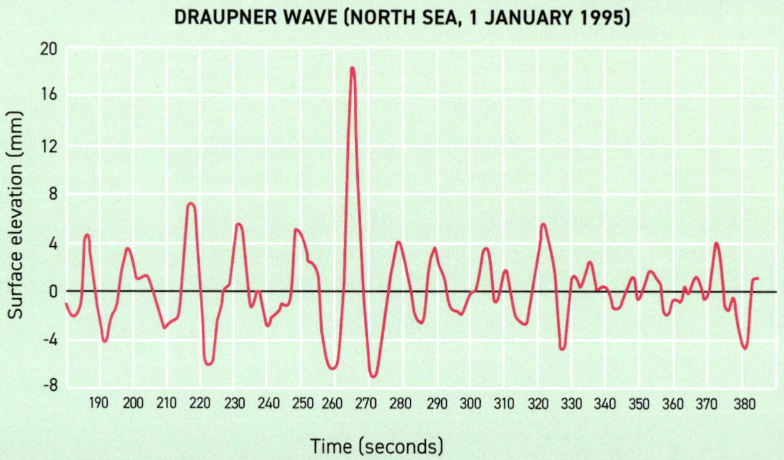

WHY WAVES TURN ROGUE

Rogue waves can occur for different reasons. High winds meeting a strong current can cause waves to merge into one giant one, as shown in the picture on the left. When waves moving in opposite directions meet, this can also generate a rogue wave, as the picture on the right demonstrates. A single huge wave can also result when small fast waves catch up with slow waves and combine.

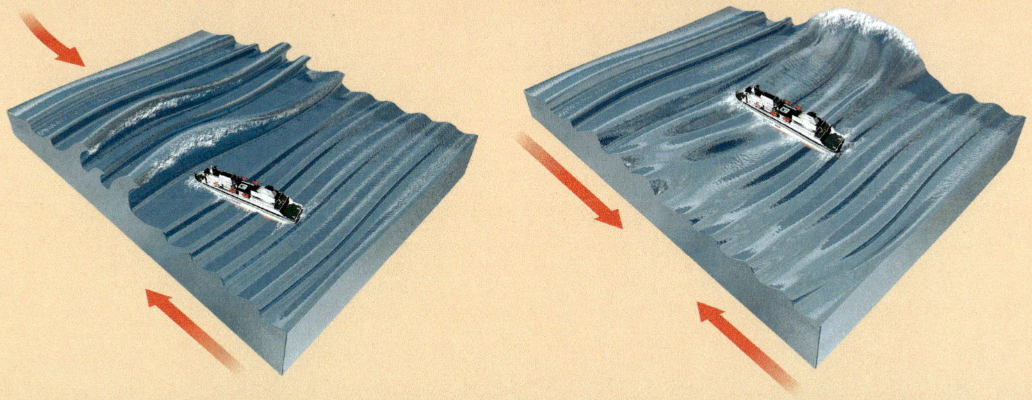

▼*Unlike a tsunami, which is generated by an earthquake or eruption, a rogue wave can be generated by wind. The lack of warning time makes it extremely hazardous.*

WATERSPOUTS

Similar to a tornado, a waterspout is a column of rotating air that forms over oceans and lakes and is a hazard to swimmers, boats and aircraft.

Despite their name, waterspouts do not spout from the water. Instead, they descend from clouds. The water inside one is mainly fresh water, formed from water vapour that has condensed from a gas to a liquid in the cloud. The diameter of a waterspout's funnel can be just a few metres across or as wide as 100 m (328 ft). The most intense waterspouts have winds of more than 100 km/h (62 mph).

CLOUD CONNECTION

Warm water and high levels of humidity, which is the amount of water vapour in the air, are key factors in creating a waterspout. The sub-tropical waters of the eastern Mediterranean Sea and the east coast of Australia are two areas where they are more common. Most waterspouts disappear within 10 minutes, but a few last up to one hour and can move onto land where they can cause more damage.

There are two types of waterspout. Fair-weather waterspouts descend from the dark bases of cumulus clouds, but they normally form at the surface of the water and spiral upwards into the cloud. They develop in light wind and are usually static. Linked with developing storm systems, they're rarely dangerous.

Tornadic waterspouts are associated with intense thunderstorms and begin as true tornadoes. They descend from cumulus or cumulonimbus clouds, and can form over water or over land before moving over water. One of the earliest records of a tornadic waterspout was in a Maltese harbour in the 16th century. At least four ships were sunk and hundreds of people lost their lives.

▶ *Because the wind direction inside a waterspout keeps changing very quickly, any boat that sails in its path could be vigorously rocked and even capsized.*

FAIR-WEATHER FORMATION

The creation of a fair-weather waterspout is shown in this picture. A dark patch becomes visible on warm water at the bottom of the column of rotating wind. A spiral pattern of dark and light bands can be seen next, followed by a ring of sea spray. A funnel grows upwards to connect with the cloud above. The waterspout collapses when the warm air flow weakens.

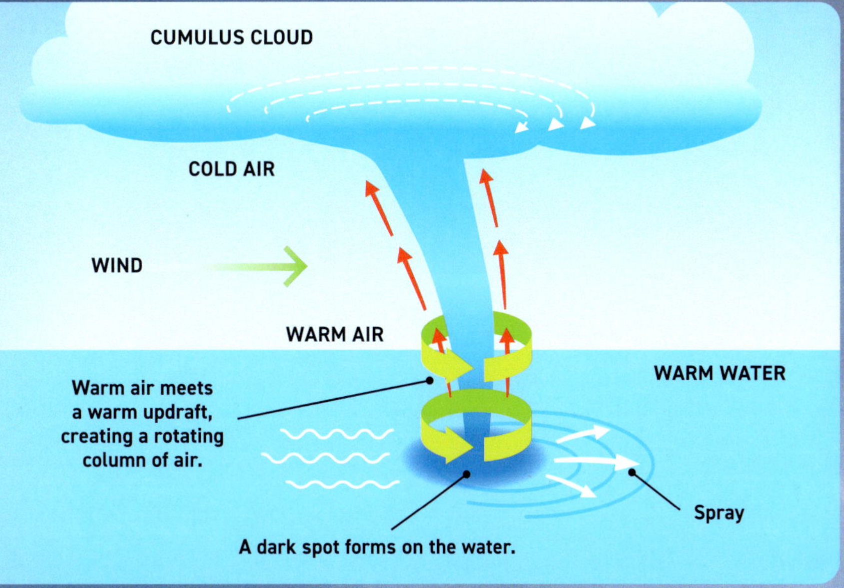

▼ *Severe thunderstorms produce the most dangerous type of waterspouts. If lightning is seen, indicating a storm, it could also be a warning that a waterspout is nearby.*

DOUBLE DANGER

Tornadic waterspouts, which develop from thunderstorms, are the type most associated with lightning. Combined with powerful winds and heavy rainfall, they can be a serious threat to shipping. In August 2024, luxury yacht the *Bayesian* sank in a fierce storm. A local fisherman in the harbour watched the lightning. Spotting a distress flare, he had to wait for a waterspout to pass before investigating, where he found the wreckage of the *Bayesian*.

SMOG

Reducing visibility as it gets thicker, this toxic haze settles over big cities around the world, harming vegetation and causing long-term health issues.

▼ *Lahore in Pakistan is one of the world's most polluted cities. Smog is worst between October and February when stubble is burnt after the rice harvest.*

Combining the words smoke and fog, smog became an increased problem when factories began burning large amounts of fossil fuels, such as coal. These release dangerous gases, including sulphur oxides, into the atmosphere. The emissions mix with water vapour in the air to create smelly, dirty sulphurous smog, which can wear away buildings and cause breathing problems and skin complaints.

FROM LONDON TO LA

One of the worst smogs of the 20th century was the one that blanketed London, England, in early December 1952. The previous weeks had been very cold, and most people heated their homes by burning coal. Smoke from the coal combined with factory pollution, and it was unable to escape because it was trapped by high pressure above the city. Light winds and moist air were ideal conditions for fog, which quickly turned to smog. Lasting four days, it was reported that cows fatally choked and around 4,000 people died.

Although sulphurous smog, also called London smog, is less common now, it is only one type. The other main kind is photochemical smog, which is sometimes called Los Angeles smog. Confusingly, it doesn't need smoke or fog to form. Yellow-brown in colour, it comes from a reaction between nitrogen oxides present in fumes from road transport and industrial plants, and carbon vapours from products like paints and pesticides. This creates the toxic gas ozone. Ozone protects us from radiation in the atmosphere, but it is harmful at ground level and damages lungs and eyes. Some big cities have passed laws to reduce smog by using smokeless fuels or creating car-free zones.

▼ *Los Angeles, USA, is surrounded by mountains, so smog cannot disperse and becomes trapped in the city. Sometimes, wildfires break out, making the smog worse.*

Daily Mail

NO. 17,642 THREE HALFPENCE — FOR QUEEN AND COMMONWEALTH — MONDAY, DECEMBER 8, 1952

LONDON EDITION

THE GREAT FOG GROWS WORSE

London streets paralysed: No buses, no taxis, no coaches, no planes

Comment

MONDAY, DECEMBER 8, 1952

THE LESSON OF ABADAN

THE pattern and purpose of Communist infiltration in the Middle East grow clearer, and it is as well that they should be recognised, as they increasingly threaten the security of Britain and the West.

The pattern has spread from Persia to Iraq, and will creep yet farther afield unless it is checked. The chief purpose is to deny oil to the West.

PIT STRIKE THREATENS CHRISTMAS STOCKINGS

Union will keep mines going

By Daily Mail Reporter

MINERS' leaders said yesterday that if 700 colliery winders carry out their strike threat the union will make sure the winding engines are kept going.

Otherwise nearly every Yorkshire miner would be out of work.

Three hours

Baby is born in lost ambulance

TUC CHIEF SNUBS MPs WHO BOOED PREMIER

MILK SUPPLIES CUT—AND BLOT OUT

Coronation regalia

▲ *This 1952 newspaper is reporting on the 'Great Smog' that severely affected London. Public transport, apart from underground trains, shut down, and the smog was so dense that people could not see their own feet.*

FIGHTING SMOG

Reducing pollution will tackle smog in the future, but water can be used to help improve surroundings immediately. Anti-smog guns, such as this one being used in New Delhi, India, spray a super-fine mist in the air. The water droplets attach to dust and other pollutants, making the particles heavier, so they fall to the ground. This leaves the air clearer.

STRANGE RAIN

Although the phrase 'raining cats and dogs' just means a heavy downpour, there has, in fact, been some peculiar precipitation of bizarre objects.

Not many people have witnessed a shower of worms, such as the one that fell on schoolchildren playing football in Galashiels, Scotland, in 2011. A more common sight is coloured rain, which is often caused by particles of dust carried by winds over thousands of kilometres. Red is perhaps the most common, and is called blood rain. However, other colours, including yellow, black, green and brown, have also been seen.

DESERT DUST

A lot of coloured rain originates in hot deserts. Every year up to 200 million tonnes (197 million tons) of fine dust particles are released in the Sahara in North Africa. A raindrop isn't pure; it forms when molecules of water bind to an airborne particle, like dust. When the drop is heavy enough, it will fall. The dust particles from the Sahara are usually yellow or red because they are rich in iron. This colours the raindrop and the dust is visible on cars, windows and the ground.

There are other sources for this unusual occurrence. Black rain can be caused by particles emitted from volcanoes or pollution. The cause isn't always obvious, however. In 2001, blood rain that stained clothes pink fell in the Indian state of Kerala. Some people thought it was fallout from meteors, but the likeliest reason seems to be fungal spores from local algae.

Animals and objects, including spiders and stones, falling as rain are an even stranger event. These are usually picked up by a waterspout or tornado before being carried and dropped. Hail (see pages 84–85) the size of golf balls falls regularly, but in 1969, actual golf balls rained down on the city of Punta Gorda in Florida. A waterspout had picked them up from a nearby golf course.

▲ *This car in Germany is covered with yellow dust from the Saharan desert. It has to be removed carefully because wiping it away scratches the vehicle's paintwork.*

▼ *The African dust turning these desert skies red can be carried by winds, blowing from west to east, to Europe or even as far as the Caribbean.*

FALLING FISH

One of the more common animals to rain from the skies is fish, as seen in this drawing of a fishy flood in Transylvania, Romania. In 2021, residents of Texarkana in the US, were amazed when fish, picked up by an updraft, began falling to the ground. In Honduras, the village of Yoro even holds an annual festival to celebrate the times fish have rained from the sky.

EXTREME WATER EVENTS

Whether it's flooding, cyclones or even just a continuous downpour, these locations have dealt with some deadly situations caused by rainfall.

Water and rain are vital to sustain life. Without them, crops cannot grow, and humans and other animals cannot survive. But too much rain can be dangerous. These places have experienced extreme precipitation. Climate change will result in more intense rainfall. With each 1°C (1.8°F) rise in air temperature, the atmosphere can hold about 7 per cent more water vapour.

Hurricane Sandy storm surge
USA, 2012

In October 2012, a huge hurricane battered the shorelines of New Jersey (seen above), as well as New York and many inland states. After causing widespread damage on Caribbean islands, Hurricane Sandy brought 161 km/h (100 mph) winds and widespread flooding to the US. It caused more than \$70 billion (£44.10 billion) worth of damage.

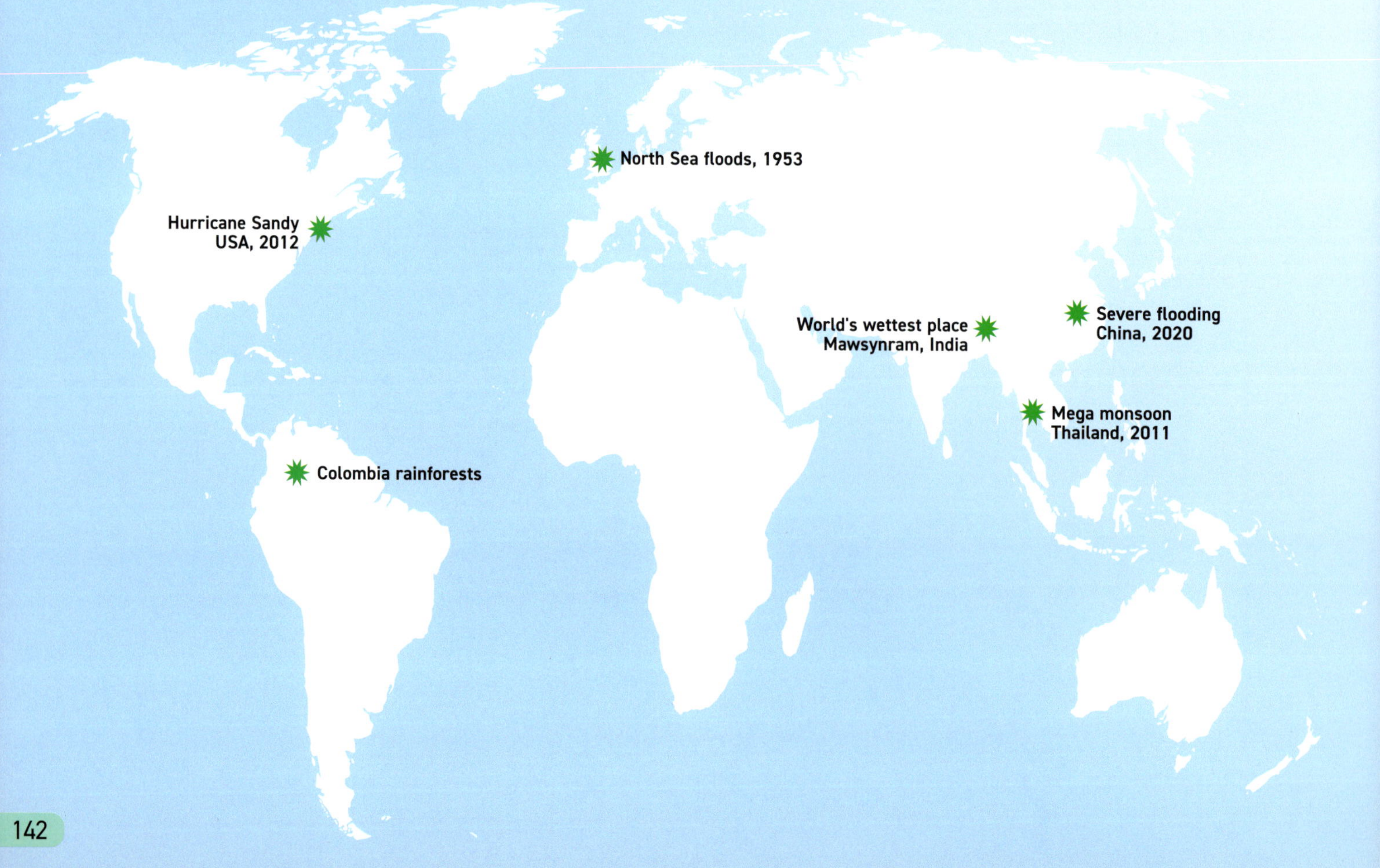

Severe flooding in China
2020

China's rainy season in June 2020 resulted in intense floods. The total precipitation in some areas was more than 1,200 mm (47 in). The flooding destroyed around 28,000 homes, and many people lost their lives. The floods affected around 63.5 million people in total – that's more than the entire population of South Africa.

North Sea floods
England, 1953

A high spring tide, severe winds and an area of low pressure combined to produce an enormous wall of North Sea water surging onto land. Waves of more than 4.9 m (16 ft) were reported. As well as England, Scotland and Belgium, the Netherlands was badly affected because much of its flooded area was below sea level.

Tropical rainforests
Colombia

This South American country's average rainfall is 3,000 mm (118 in) every year – more than three times the average worldwide. This causes frequent flooding, which has been made worse where the rainforest has been cut down. Many wetlands, where excess water from rivers normally flows, are now used for farming or housing, and often end up underwater.

Mega monsoon
Thailand, 2011

In one of the worst monsoon seasons in modern history, Thailand saw 65 of its 77 provinces declared flood disaster zones in 2011. The record rainfall submerged over 30,000 km^2 (11,600 sq miles) of land, claiming 800 lives and causing around £30 billion of damage.

World's wettest place
Mawsynram, India

The village Mawsynram holds the world record for the highest average annual rainfall. The average yearly rainfall across the whole of India is 1,250 mm (49 in), but Mawsynram sees nearly 12,000 mm (472 in) of rain, most of which falls during the monsoon season.

6 PREPARING FOR THE FUTURE

NEW FORECASTING TECHNOLOGY

Weather predictions are made using recording stations, radar systems and supercomputers with ever more accurate AI modelling systems.

Thousands of automatic weather recording stations observe the weather at or near the Earth's surface, and exchange information globally. They measure atmospheric pressure, temperature, rainfall and wind speed. Observatories use radar to track changes to the atmosphere, while weather balloons carry instruments high into the sky. Meteorologists analyse the data to help forecast the weather.

▲ *An automatic weather recording station, Switzerland. The stations collect data from weather sensors and rain gauges, and send it through a network to meteorologists.*

SUPERCOMPUTERS AND AI

Modern forecasting technologies focus on computer modelling using supercomputers. These are expensive, powerful computers that make calculations based on a global weather model. They use billions of worldwide weather observations and knowledge from physics about how the weather works to predict what is likely to happen. Over the last decade, AI, using machine learning techniques, has been adopted for weather forecasting. It can run on a laptop rather than a costly supercomputer, working much faster and using far less energy. The AI model is trained on 40 years of data and existing global weather models. Like the older models, AI forecasting is less accurate the further ahead it predicts, because even with all the available data, it's hard to predict changes in the atmosphere. AI can forecast large-scale changes, such as low or high pressure, but is not accurate at a small scale, such as a local rain shower. AI forecasting may predict a hurricane, but not the wind strength, so it is difficult to warn people about how much damage will be caused. However, AI models are improving rapidly, making them powerful tools for forecasting.

▲ *Observatory weather stations, such as this one, use radar to monitor the lower layers of the atmosphere and can forecast storms.*

WEATHER FORECASTING

Meteorologists analyse data from weather stations, radar and satellites (see page 148), and send short and long-range weather forecasts to the public and government. They issue severe weather warnings and provide advice specially for weather-dependent industries, such as farming and airlines. Meteorologists also do research to improve our understanding of changing climate.

▼ *A meteorologist at the National Weather Service office in Hastings, Nebraska, monitors weather conditions.*

AI AND RESOURCES

AI modelling for weather forecasting uses much less energy than supercomputers, but powering AI systems still requires precious resources. Huge data centres are built to run and train the AI models, with servers and storage drives that need electricity, along with water for cooling systems to stop them overheating. It is best if the energy comes from renewable sources (see page 94).

◀ *Meteorologists in Kansas, USA, launch a weather balloon into a thunderstorm. It carries instruments to obtain data on temperature, pressure, wind speed and electrical fields.*

SATELLITES AND NATURAL DISASTERS

Satellites help scientists to forecast the weather. They monitor the conditions on Earth and supply data to predict natural disasters and provide warnings.

Orbiting around Earth, weather satellites observe clouds, rain, snow and storm patterns worldwide and send data. Polar orbiting satellites fly around 850 km (about 530 miles) above the Earth, passing over both poles several times a day. They take around 100 minutes to do a full orbit. About 35,800 km (22,200 miles) above the Equator, geostationary satellites stay above the same spot on Earth, orbiting it once every 24 hours.

USING WEATHER SATELLITES

Polar-orbiting satellites provide high-quality images of Earth. Their orbit is timed with the Sun, so they observe the same area at the same local time every day. They collect data on the atmosphere, temperature and rainfall over the whole Earth. Geostationary satellites take a photo of the Earth in the same place, every 5–30 minutes. Weather satellites collect information on changing conditions, such as ice cover and ocean currents. They detect sandstorms and the effects of pollution. When natural disasters occur, they track the hazards – for example, the path of a tornado or the smoke from wildfires.

▶ *Geostationary satellites orbit at the same rate as Earth spins, so they remain above the same place. They monitor the weather in real time.*

MONITORING VOLCANIC ACTIVITY

Satellites can check for volcanic activity anywhere in the world, however remote. They observe changes in heat and a volcano's shape that may mean it is about to erupt. If volcanic activity occurs, an alert system detects it within hours and can issue warnings. Following an eruption, satellite technology predicts where volcanic ash clouds will spread, so people can escape.

◀ *A satellite image of an eruption from the side of Mount Etna, Italy, in 2018.*

EARTHQUAKE ACTIVITY

Interferograms show how the ground moves during an earthquake. They are created from radar signals sent by satellites. The satellite takes a radar image of the ground. Later, it takes another one of the same place. If the ground has moved, the signal changes. The shift is shown by rainbow-coloured patterns of lines, with each colour marking a specific amount of movement.

▶ *Using interferograms from a polar-orbiting satellite, scientists saw how the ground moved in the 2014 California earthquake.*

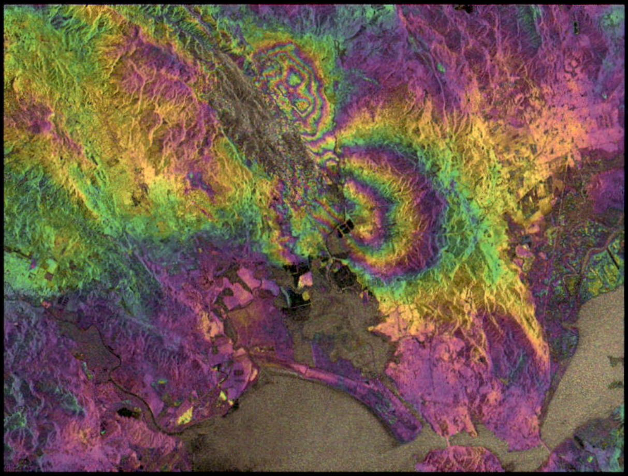

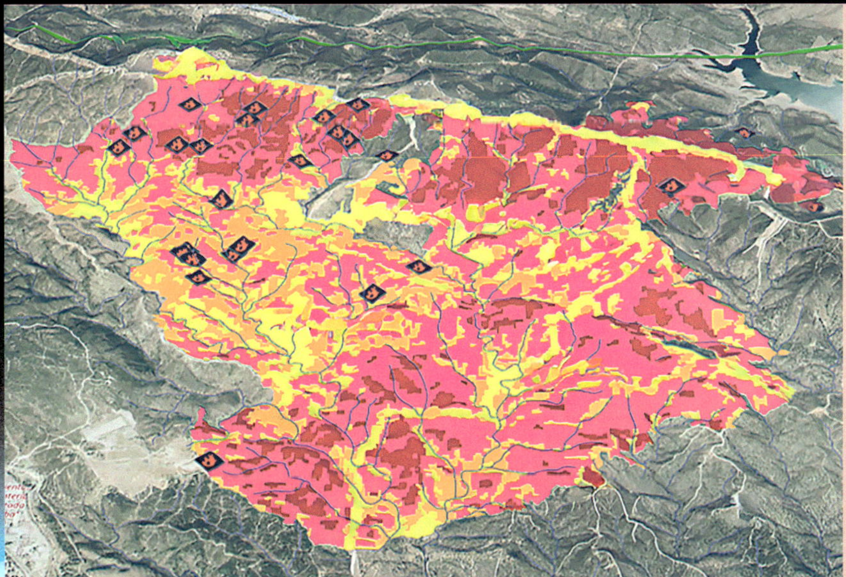

RISK AND RECOVERY MAPS

This risk and recovery map shows the damage caused in Spain after the 2025 wildfires. It comes from the European Union's Copernicus emergency management service. The service observes Earth and provides radar and optical satellite images (these catch the sunlight that bounces off oceans, land and buildings and turns it into photos). After a natural disaster, risk maps help European countries to prevent future disasters, prepare for emergencies and adapt to climate change.

COUNTERING THE CAUSES OF CLIMATE CHANGE

We can limit climate change by switching to renewable energy forms that limit greenhouse gases. Some key sources are the Sun, wind and Earth's heat.

Solar power harnesses energy from sunlight using panels or mirrors to provide heat and electricity. Wind power is generated by using turbines that capture the energy of moving air. Geothermal power taps into Earth's internal heat, working much like a steam engine. The shift to renewable energy can help temper the rise in the number and intensity of extreme weather events that cause so much damage.

SOLAR AND WIND POWER

Many countries invest in solar and wind farms. China has the biggest projects of both types, although it still relies heavily on fossil fuels, too. The Gonghe Talatan Solar Park in Qinghai Province is situated at high altitude, an ideal place for catching sunlight. The solar farm creates around 3.2 gigawatts (GW) of power – enough energy to power around 3 million UK homes. China also has a giant onshore wind farm: the 10-GW Gansu Wind Farm, which is near the Gobi Desert. With more than 7,000 wind turbines, it creates enough electricity to power a small country. Even so, China still gets less than a quarter of its overall power from wind and solar. Denmark has the highest percentage, with 70 per cent of its energy from wind and solar.

▲ *A 2,383-km (1,480-mile) electricity line brings power from the remote Gansu Wind Farm to urban China.*

▼ *This solar energy plant is near Seville, southern Spain, which has at least 10 hours of sunshine daily from May to mid-August.*

GEOTHERMAL POWER

Below Earth's surface is magma – extremely hot, liquid rock. In parts of the world, steam from magma escapes through cracks in Earth's crust to the surface. The heat from rocks can be used for power. The steam travels in pipes to a geothermal power plant to make electricity. Likewise, geothermal heat pump systems can heat buildings in winter. In summer, heat is pumped out of the building and back into the ground. More than 20 countries use geothermal power. The USA produces the most. With about 25 active volcanoes and many hot springs, around a quarter of Iceland's electricity comes from geothermal power, heating 90 per cent of the country's homes.

◀ *Hellisheidi geothermal power station in Iceland. As well as producing electricity, it supplies hot water to the capital Reykjavik for heating homes and industries.*

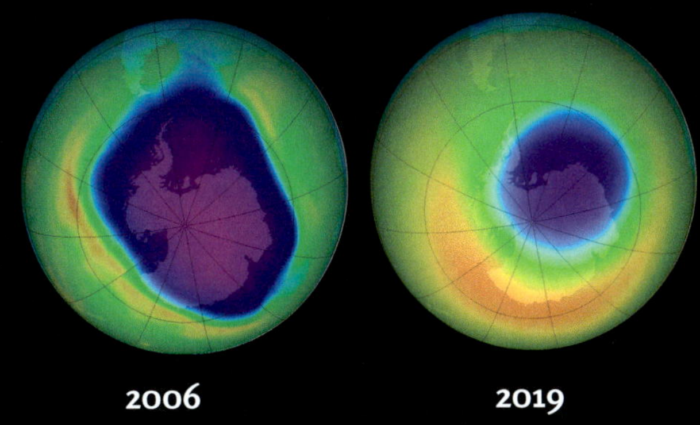

OZONE LAYER 'HOLE'

The ozone layer is like the Earth's sunscreen, protecting it from ultraviolet (UV) radiation that makes skin burn. It absorbs 98 per cent of the most harmful UV rays. In 1974, scientists realised that chemicals called chlorofluorocarbons (CFCs) in many goods, especially fridges, were destroying the ozone layer. In 1987, countries worldwide agreed to gradually stop making CFCs. Luckily, other chemicals were found to replace them. The images show that the ozone layer 'hole' above Antarctica slowly recovered after 2006.

NATURAL DISASTER DEFENCES

Special building techniques and natural defences can reduce the impact of natural disasters such as earthquakes, tsunamis and floods.

Many countries with a high tsunami risk build walls and other defences to reduce their impact as well as shelters on high ground. In Japan, after the powerful Tohoku earthquake and tsunami of 2011, the government built around 400 km (250 miles) of seawalls along the coast. The walls do not completely block the waves, but they allow people more time to escape when they hear the early-warning siren.

NATURAL DEFENCES

Alongside the seawalls in Japan, around 9 million trees help to keep the sand dunes stable. The trees and sand dunes absorb some of a tsunami's power, reducing the speed and height of the waves, so the floodwaters do not travel as fast or as far inland. The higher and wider the sand dunes are, the more energy they absorb. Some countries around the Indian and Pacific Oceans have coral reefs. They stretch from the low tide mark into deeper water, like an underwater wall. The force of the waves weakens as it spreads over the rough surface of the coral. Many tropical and subtropical countries use mangrove forests as a defence against tsunamis. The trees' thick trunks and twisted branches slow down the waves.

▲ *These concrete tetrapod blocks are commonly used in Japan to protect the coastline from wave damage. The water flows around the shapes, reducing the wave energy.*

▼ *In Ban Tha Din Daeng, Thailand, the community has restored mangrove forests swept away by the 2004 Indian Ocean tsunami, to protect against future tsunamis.*

▲ *A demonstration in Kathmandu, Nepal, of how a normal house collapses in an earthquake shows, people they should build earthquake-proof homes.*

BULDING FOR EARTHQUAKES

In an earthquake, most deaths and injuries are caused by buildings collapsing. There are several ways to design buildings to reduce earthquake damage, and some countries have rules to ensure buildings are earthquake-proof. A flexible steel skeleton can be added to concrete buildings so that they can move and return to their normal shape. Buildings can also have 'base isolation' systems, with thick rubber layers to separate the building from its foundations. In an earthquake, the rubber absorbs the force. These methods save lives and reduce damage to property.

TSUNAMI TOWERS

When people hear a tsunami warning, they need to quickly move to high ground – the wave could arrive in under half an hour. But they may live several kilometres from a hill. Tsunami Vertical Evacuation Structures, or tsunami towers, are taller than the level of the highest waves. They are constructed near the coast so people can reach shelter easily. Made from concrete or steel frames, they are strong enough to remain standing in an earthquake and a tsunami. During the 2011 Tohoku tsunami, these towers provided refuge, saving many lives.

▼ *A tsunami tower, Ko Phayam island, Thailand. The Thai coast has a warning system and many shelters near popular beaches.*

FLOOD DEFENCE

Formed of over 100 islands, Venice is at risk of flooding due to rising sea levels. It is protected by a flood defence system that was tested using a model (right). There are concrete barriers at the three sea entrances. When not in use, they lie on the seabed. If the tide reaches a certain level, the barriers rise to stop seawater flowing into Venice.

GLOSSARY

The following pages explain most of the technical terms that are used in this book. Where a definition includes words in **bold**, it means that these words have entries of their own.

AI
Artificial Intelligence, or computers that can learn.

Altitude
The height of something relative to sea or ground level.

Anticyclone
An area of high air pressure that is often accompanied by calm weather. It is the opposite of a **cyclone**.

Asteroid
Lumps of space rock, ranging in size from just over 1 m (3 ft) across to 1,000 km (620 miles) across.

Atmosphere
The layer of gases held around a planet by **gravity**.

Atmospheric cells
Large, global circulation patterns of air. There are three kinds – Hadley, Polar and Ferrel.

Barometer
A scientific instrument used to measure air pressure.

Bedrock
Solid rock found under soil and other loose surface material.

Black ice
Ice formed on roads and paths that is hard to see because of its transparency.

Boreal forests
Forests – typically of conifer trees – that grow in far northern regions.

Convergent plate boundary
A tectonic boundary where two plates collide.

Cyclone
An area of low air pressure that usually comes with cold, wet and windy weather. It is the opposite of an **anticyclone**.

Deforestation
The destruction of a forest and conversion of the land for another purpose.

Derecho
A widespread wind storm that starts as a thunderstorm and causes damage over more than 386 km (250 miles).

Dirty thunderstorm
Lightning generated within a volcanic ash cloud.

Divergent plate boundary
A tectonic boundary where two plates move apart.

Dormant
A volcano that is not currently erupting, but is also not yet extinct.

Epicentre
Point on the planet surface directly above an earthquake's origin point.

Equator
An imaginary line around the middle of the planet that divides Earth into Northern and Southern hemispheres. It influences surface currents and sea surface temperatures.

Erosion
The action of rock wearing away.

Eruption
The geological event when materials, such as gas, ash and lava, are expelled from a volcano.

Extinct
A volcano that scientists believe won't erupt again.

Fault line
A place on Earth's surface where the division between two tectonic plates can be seen.

Fire devil
A whirlwind made up of fire or ash. Also known as a fire whirl or fire tornado.

Floodplain
An area of land next to a river that becomes submerged when the river floods.

Focus
The location that an earthquake originates from, usually deep inside the rocky layer around Earth.

Geyser
A hot spring that sometimes erupts, forcing hot water and steam into the air.

Glacier
A river of ice formed from mountain snow that flows slowly downhill.

Gravity
The force that pulls objects towards the centre of a planet.

Greenhouse gases
Gases such as carbon dioxide and methane that trap the Sun's heat in Earth's **atmosphere**.

High-pressure system
Associated with nice weather, an area of air that is denser and heavier. Also known as **anticyclone**.

Ice shove
The pile up of ice on a shore by a lake or ocean caused by strong winds and differences in temperature.

Industrial Revolution
Period of time that started at the end of the 18th century when industry replaced other economies, increasing the usage of fossil fuels.

Infrastructure
Buildings, facilities, roads and power supplies needed for society to operate.

Karst
A limestone landscape that features caves and sinkholes created by water eroding the rock.

Lahar
Volcanic mudflow.

Lava
The name given to **magma** when it has erupted from a volcano.

Limestone
A sedimentary rock.

Lithosphere
The outer rocky layer of Earth, composed of the crust and part of the upper **mantle**.

Low-pressure system
An area where air is lighter and less dense than that around it. Also known as **cyclone**.

Magma
Molten rocks created by the **mantle** melting in subduction zones where **tectonic plates** meet.

Mangrove forests
Coastal ecosystems that work as natural flood defences.

Mantle
The layer of rock between Earth's crust and core.

Meteorological
Relating to the atmosphere and weather.

Moment magnitude scale
Method of measuring the intensity of earthquakes.

Nuclear fusion
The reaction within the Sun that creates heat and light.

Ozone
A layer of gas that protects Earth from UV rays.

Polar
Relating to the areas around the North and South Poles.

Pollution
Harmful substances introduced into the natural environment.

Precipitation
Anything that falls from clouds: rain, snow, sleet and hail.

Pyroclastic flow
The mixture of gas, solids and liquids that flow from a volcano at high speed.

Radiation
The movement of energy in waves through space.

Richter scale
Method of measuring earthquakes. Now generally surpassed by the **Moment magnitude scale**.

Ring of Fire
Area around the Pacific Ocean that is home to most of Earth's active volcanoes.

Satellites
Objects orbiting a planet. Human-made satellites help with weather and disaster forecasting.

Sea level
Average height of the sea's surface, it is used to measure **altitude**.

Seismic swarm
Cluster of small earthquakes in a particular area that don't accompany a larger shock.

Seismograph
Instrument that records tremors and earthquakes.

Supercell
A type of severe thunderstorm.

Tectonic plate
Part of the **lithosphere** that is broken into smaller pieces, or plates.

Temperate
A climate of mild temperatures.

Transform plate boundary
A tectonic boundary where two plates slide past each other.

Tremor
A small earthquake.

Tropical
A hot, humid climate.

Twister
Another name for a tornado.

Volcanologist
A scientist who studies volcanic activity.

INDEX

A

B

C

D

E

M

N

O

P

QR

S

ACKNOWLEDGEMENTS

The publisher would like to thank the following for permission to reproduce their material.
Key: **b = bottom, c = centre, m = middle, l = left, r = right, t = top**

4l Martin Rietze / Science Photo Library; 4r Nagel Photography / Shutterstock; 5l Gabriella N. Baez / Bloomberg / Getty; 5r Mark MacEwen / naturepl.com; 6 NASA Earth Observatory image by Lauren Dauphin, using VIIRS data from NASA EOSDIS LANCE, GIBS/Worldview, and the Suomi National Polar-orbiting Partnership; 8-9 Herve Conge / Science Photo Library; 10 Dynamo; 10-11 Naeblys / Shutterstock; 11 Loic Poidevin / naturepl.com; 12 Arnaldur Sigurðarson / Alamy; 12-13 Zzvet / Dreamstime; 13t Kevin Schafer / Getty; 13m Kevin Schafer / Minden / naturepl.com; 14t Mark Williamson / Science Photo Library; 14b Newscom / Alamy Live News; 14-15 STR/AFP via Getty Images; 15 Dynamo; 16tl ART Collection / Alamy; 16tr home for heroes / Shutterstock; 16-17 Ozgur Donmaz / Getty; 17t US Geological Survey / Science Photo Library; 17m Wikipedia / European Union, Copernicus Digital Elevation Model contains modified Copernicus Sentinel data 2025; 17b Andrea Danti / Shutterstock; 18-19 Xinhua / Alamy Live News; 20-21 WENN Rights Ltd / Alamy; 21 Monica Schroeder / Science Photo Library; 22t International Tsunami Information Centre (ITIC); 22b RLawall / Shutterstock; 23t Jane Rix / Alamy; 23m James Hackland / Alamy; 24-25 Mark Garlick / Science Photo Library; 25t Mark Garlick / Science Photo Library; 25b Fran Arna / Amazing Aerial Agency / Science Photo Library; 26t BlueRingMedia / Shutterstock; 27ml Richard Roscoe/Stocktrek Images / Getty; 27mr Greg Vaughn / Alamy; 28t Arctic Images / Alamy; 28m Rainer Lesniewski / Shutterstock; 28b Patrick Landmann / Science Photo Library; 28-29 Sergey Gorshkov / naturepl.com; 29t Erlend Haarberg / naturepl.com; 30-31 Martin Rietze / Science Photo Library; 32-33 Matthew Oldfield / Science Photo Library; 33t Finnbarr Webster / Getty; 33m US Army National Guard / Science Photo Library; 33b Dynamo; 34b Brian Skerry / Minden / naturepl.com; 34-35 PA Images / Alamy; 35b Dynamo; 36-37 Martin Rietze / Science Photo Library; 38-39 David Parker / Science Photo Library; 39t Science Photo Library; 39ml serpeblu / Shutterstock; 39mr Wikipedia / Leonid Kulik, the expedition to the Tunguska event; 40t Keystone-France/Gamma-Keystone via Getty Images; 40b Yusiki / Shutterstock; 41tl Frans Delian / Shutterstock; 41tr Prof. Stewart Lowther / Science Photo Library; 41ml Bertrand Parres/AFP via Getty Images; 41mr Elizaveta Becker/ullstein bild via Getty Images; 41b imago/Xinhua / Alamy; 42-43 temizyurek / Getty; 44 CHAOSPHERE / Shutterstock; 44-45 NASA / SDO / Science Photo Library; 45 Akimov Igor / Shutterstock; 46-47b leolintang / Shutterstock; 46-47t NASA / Science Photo Library; 47ma elenabs / iStock / Getty; 48-49 Shao-chun Wang / Dreamstime; 48-49t Dynamo / CHAOSPHERE / Shutterstock; 49tr VectorMine / Dreamstime; 50-51 johnwoodcock / Getty; 50tr ekvals / Getty; 50mb MikeMareen / iStock / Getty; 50b Cid Guedes / iStock / Getty; 51tl Bruno Ismael Da Silva Alves / Dreamstime; 51tr Md Zakir Hossain / iStock / Getty; 51bl Piyaset / Shutterstock; 51br Juergen Freund / naturepl.com; 52-53 Roy Mangersnes / naturepl.com; 54-55t Science History Images / Alamy; 54-55b happy8790 / iStock / Getty; 55t Dynamo; 55m SeppFriedhuber / iStock / Getty; 56-57t Jaden Schaul / Shutterstock; 56-57b Sergio Hanquet / naturepl.com; 57 Dynamo; 58t Thichaa / Shutterstock; 58m Jo-Anne McArthur / WeAnimals / naturepl.com; 58-59 Jeff Vanuga / naturepl.com; 59tl Adrian Davies / naturepl.com; 59tr Dr Neil Overy / Science Photo Library; 59m Mimadeo / Alamy; 60-61 ZUMA Press, Inc. / Alamy; 62-63t Tui De Roy / Minden / naturepl.com; 62-63b Carol & Mike Werner / Science Photo Library; 63 B.A.E. Inc. / Alamy; 64ml Paul Sequeira / Science Photo Library; 64m Ashley Cooper / Science Photo Library; 64r Dynamo; 64bl Alex Mustard / naturepl.com; 65t Gary Braasch / naturepl.com; 65b Franco Banfi / naturepl.com; 66 NurPhoto / Getty; 66-67t Lin Yunlong/Zhejiang Daily Press Group/VCG via Getty Images; 66-67b NASA / Goddard Space Flight Center Scientific Visualization Studio; 67 zombiu26 / Shutterstock; 68t Steven Group / Shutterstock; 68b Yusiki / Shutterstock; 69t ABDELHAK SENNA/AFP via Getty Images; 69ml Cat Downie / Shutterstock; 69mr NASA Earth Observatory images by Wanmei Liang, using Landsat data from the U.S. Geological Survey and MODIS data from NASA; 69b Antonin Albert / Shutterstock; 70-71 Guy Edwardes / 2020VISION / naturepl.com; 72-73 Johner Images / Alamy; 72 Kichigin / Shutterstock; 73t paul weston/ Alamy; 73m Dynamo; 74-75 The Asahi Shimbun via Getty Images; 75t wwing / iStock / Getty; 75b NickJulia / Shutterstock; 76-77 Rick Friedman/rick@rickfriedman.com/Corbis via Getty Images; 76l Sandra Bartocha / naturepl.com; 76b Nadine Mitchell / Alamy; 76r Aiphotographic / iStock / Getty; 77t Olga Aniven / Shutterstock; 77m Hurst Photo / Shutterstock; 77b Bryan and Cherry Alexander / naturepl.com; 78-79 Nagel Photography / Shutterstock; 78-79t Laurent Fady / Alamy; 79 Michael Tatman / Alamy; 80-81 Anton Petrus / Getty; 82-83 justkgoomm / Shutterstock; 82t Narongsak Nagadhana / Shutterstock; 83t Jaromir Chalabala / Alamy; 83b NASA Earth Observatory, Joshua Stevens / Science Photo Library; 84-85 AlesVeluscek / Getty; 84-85t Mike Hollingshead / Science Photo Library; 85t VectorMine / Shutterstock; 85b Luca Piccini Basile / iStock / Getty; 86-87 Kirill Skorobogatko / Shutterstock; 87 Dynamo; 88-89 Lee Cohen / Getty; 88t PHILIPPE DESMAZES/AFP via Getty Images; 88b Ashley Cooper / Science Photo Library; 89t Lilkin / iStock / Getty; 89b Yves Lanceau / naturepl.com; 90t Bryan and Cherry Alexander / naturepl.com; 90b Yusiki / Shutterstock; 91tl Kyodo / Newscom / Alamy Live News; 91tr Wikipedia / Arctic and Antarctic Research Institute; 91ml imageBROKER.com / Alamy; 91b Chisanu LIENGPAN / Alamy; 91mr Image Source Limited / Alamy; 92-93 Warren Faidley / Getty; 94-95 Orsolya Haarberg / naturepl.com; 94t Artur Synenko / Shutterstock; 95t Dynamo; 95m Jan Wlodarczyk / Alamy; 96m ZhakYaroslav / Shutterstock; 96b Lester Balajadia / Shutterstock; 97l Designua / Shutterstock; 97tr Premium Stock Photography GmbH / Alamy; 97mr Antero Aaltonen / Shutterstock; 97br Geoffrey Robinson / Alamy; 98-99 Guy Edwardes / naturepl.com; 99t zelvan / Shutterstock; 99b IanDagnall Computing / Alamy; 100-101 Tsado / NASA / Alamy; 100t NASA Earth Observatory image by Lauren Dauphin, using VIIRS data from NASA EOSDIS LANCE, GIBS/Worldview, and the Suomi National Polar-orbiting Partnership; 100b VectorMine / Shutterstock; 101 VectorMine / Shutterstock; 102-103 Gabriella N. Baez/Bloomberg / Getty; 102t Dynamo; 103t Jim Reed / Science Photo Library; 103ml Bilanol / Shutterstock; 103mr Jim Edds / Science Photo Library; 104-105 Reed Timmer / Science Photo Library; 105t Monica Schroeder / Science Photo Library; 105b Dynamo; 106-107 Laura Hedien / Getty; 108-109 US Army Photo / Alamy; 108t John Sirlin / Alamy; 108m Jim Reed Photography / Science Photo Library; 109m European Space Agency / ATG MediaLab / Science Photo Library; 110-111 John Sirlin / Alamy; 110-111t Jack Reynolds / Getty; 111 Abstract Aerial Art / Getty; 112t GRANGER - Historical Picture Archive / Alamy; 112b Yusiki / Shutterstock; 113tl DAVID L. NELSON/ AFP via Getty Images; 113tr © City of Phoenix/ZUMA Press Wire / Alamy; 113ml Pete Pattisson/ZUMAPRESS.com / Alamy; 113mr Benjamin Krain / Getty Images; 113b Rolls Press/Popperfoto via Getty Images; 114-115 Theo Bosboom / naturepl.com; 116-117 Platon Anton / Shutterstock; 117tl Cavan Images / Alamy; 117tr Dynamo; 117ml Jacques Giraud / 500p x/ Getty; 117mr Dynamo; 117bl r.s.panov / 500px / Getty; 117br Dynamo; 118tr Pla2na / iStock / Getty; 118ml Stephen Burt / Science Photo Library; 118mr artisteer / iStock / Getty; 118b Annandistock / iStock / Getty; 119t Trent Abbott / iStock / Getty; 119ml Dusty Roads / Shutterstock; 119mr LiuNian / iStock / Getty; 119m George Post / Science Photo Library; 119bl Yes058 Montree Nanta / Shutterstock; 119br Bruce Robinson / Alamy; 120-121 Simon Fraser / Science Photo Library; 121t Peter M.Miller / Science Photo Library; 121b Storyet / Shutterstock; 122-123 Roger Hill / Science Photo Library; 124-125 Mark MacEwen / naturepl.com; 124 AP Tolang / Shutterstock; 125t DEWIRA / AFP via Getty; 125b weerastudio / Shutterstock; 126-127 victor yankee / Shutterstock; 126 Mark Williamson / Science Photo Library; 127t Dynamo; 127 Ashley Cooper / Science Photo Library; 128t Ashley Cooper / Science Photo Library; 128m David Ramos / Getty; 128b robertharding / Alamy; 129t Environment Agency / Managing future flood risk and Thames Barrier: Thames Estuary 2100; 129m Colin Edwards, John Birdsall Social Issues Photo Library / Science Photo Library; 129b Pulsar Images / Alamy; 130-131 thianchai sitthikongsak / Getty; 132-133 Jim Edds / Science Photo Library; 132 Robyn Beck / AFP via Getty; 133 Dynamo; 134-135 Lemke Images / Shutterstock; 134t By Katsushika Hokusai - Metropolitan Museum of Art: entry 45434; 134b Dynamo; 135t Mikkel Juul Jensen / Science Photo Library; 136-137 Steve Harris / Alamy; 137t Dynamo; 137b swa182 / Shutterstock; 138-139 GIPHOTOSTOCK / Science Photo Library; 138-139t Syed Murtaza Ali / AFP / Getty; 139t John Frost Newspapers / Alamy; 139m Money SHARMA / AFP / Getty; 140-141 grafisphos / Alamy; 140-141t Edgar G. Biehle / Alamy; 141 Ken Welsh / Deesign Pictures / Science Phoro Library; 142t NASA Image Collection / Alamy; 142b Yusiki / Shutterstock; 143tl Liu Zhankun / China News Service via Getty; 143tr stockphoto mania / Shutterstock; 143m Juancho Torres / Anadolu Agency via Getty; 143mr Subhendu Sarkar / LightRocket via Getty; 143bl CO ZEYLEMAKER / AFP via Getty; 144-145 Richard Herrmann / Minden / naturepl.com; 146-147 Jim Reed / Science Photo Library; 146t Alistair Scott / Alamy; 146m RAWS / Shutterstock; 147tl Ryan McGinnis / Alamy; 147tr MarutStudio / Shutterspace; 148-149 ESA / Mlabspace; 149t Geopix / Alamy; 149m Copernicus data (2014) / ESA / PPO.labs / Norut / COMET-SEOM Insarap study; 149b Copernicus EU; 150-151 Ashley Cooper / Science Photo Library; 150t Matyas Rehak / Dreamstime; 151t NASA Earth Observatory; 151m Ashley Cooper / Science Photo Library; 152t Andy Crump / Science Photo Library; 152b Khachachart Anontaseeha / Dreamstime; 153tl Xinhua / Alamy Live News; 153mr Aliaksandr Mazurkevich / Alamy; 153b Volker Steger / Science Photo Library